Diary of a North London Lad

Diary of a North London Lad

Tony Shelton

authorHOUSE®

AuthorHouse™
1663 Liberty Drive
Bloomington, IN 47403
www.authorhouse.com
Phone: 1-800-839-8640

First published by AuthorHouse   08/04/2011

ISBN: 978-1-4567-8656-4 (sc)
ISBN: 978-1-4567-8655-7 (ebk)

Printed in the United States of America

Any people depicted in stock imagery provided by Thinkstock are models, and such images are being used for illustrative purposes only.
Certain stock imagery © Thinkstock.

This book is printed on acid-free paper.

Because of the dynamic nature of the Internet, any web addresses or links contained in this book may have changed since publication and may no longer be valid. The views expressed in this work are solely those of the author and do not necessarily reflect the views of the publisher, and the publisher hereby disclaims any responsibility for them.

This book is for
Rebecca, Serena and Lucinda with love.

Prologue

Round the table, in varying stages of intoxication, were eight of us, celebrating a milestone birthday. Well lubricated with about ten bottles of wine, gin and tonics, vodka and cokes, and then brandy, we all settled down to watch a film. One of the male guests was making a very rude suggestion to one of the female guests, while another male guest was being presented with a very rude book, the pages of which were all blank except for two. My eyes eventually drifted back to the screen, but my mind was beginning to wander—and wonder how the years had panned out, and what a journey it had been.

Chapter One

I was born on 24th January, 1940 in Harefield Road, Tottenham. This was my maternal grandparents' house, but I remember nothing of it, as we moved to 'Rockville', 165 Victoria Road, Wood Green when I was two. As Dad (Ernest George Shelton) could not afford to buy it, 'Rockville' was rented; it was a long, narrow, Victorian terraced house with a cellar, then three rooms, scullery and outside toilet on the ground floor and three rooms, kitchen, bathroom and separate toilet upstairs. Most rooms had a mouthpiece set into the wall so that servants could be summoned from the control room on the ground floor, but as any servants had long disappeared by the time we moved in, the system fell into disrepair. Among early memories were being wheeled down Victoria Road towards Rhodes Avenue in a pram by my grandmother (my Father's mother Jessie, who lived with us), milk being delivered by Paddy the milkman in his horse-drawn cart and coal being delivered by the coalman in his horse-drawn cart. Another regular visitor (though not in a horse-drawn cart) was the lugubrious Mr. Clarke, the landlord, who called once a month to collect the rent. He was always dressed in a dark grey overcoat and a dark grey homburg. One day he offered to sell Dad the house for £500. Dad couldn't raise that sort of money, but Mr. Clarke was persistent; it would take him another twenty years, however, to effect the sale. Either he was insistent on selling to Dad, or nobody else was interested in buying.

The Second World War had started just before I was born, and I remember being given a weekly scrub down in a tin bath in front of the fire, being put to bed in an Anderson shelter, my parents looking horrific in gas masks, the eerie sound of air raid sirens, and the frightening noises of the aeroplanes and the bombs they were dropping. Although we never suffered a direct hit during the bombing, houses all around us did, and now bungalows in Victoria Road testify to where houses were demolished. Mum, (Ada Rose Pace), had been born in October 1908 and Dad in May, 1909. They had first met at a Conservative club in Tottenham, and were married in October 1938. In April 1942, Dad was called up to serve in the Royal Engineers, where he stayed until 1946, having been awarded the British Empire medal.

At some time around 1942 or '43 Mum and I were evacuated to Leicester; memories are somewhat sketchy, but I vaguely remember a boarding house just outside the town centre, and getting whooping cough. On our return, when I was four, I was sent to Elmsleigh School, just round the corner in Alexandra Park Road, but I didn't last very long; after six weeks, I was expelled for being a bad influence on the other children. (I never did discover what form this influence took). Far from being a bad influence, I regarded myself as a bit of a softy. Listening to the radio one day, I burst into tears when the sparrow admitted killing Cock Robin with a bow and arrow! Indeed, it was my imaginary friend Giggygog, an evil bastard, who was the troublemaker—whenever anything went missing or got broken; it was always Giggygog's fault—never mine.

VE Day, 8th May 1945 was the day the German forces surrendered and the war was over.

Mum and Dad both played the piano and loved classical music. I fondly remember listening to Tchaikovsky's Piano Concerto no.1 and Litolff's Concerto Symphonique, both rousing piano pieces. I also remember hearing Sparky's Magic Piano on the radio—wonderful! (I wonder how it would be appreciated by today's youngsters?) One day, I was looking through the sheet music in the piano stool when I discovered a copy of Razzle magazine, which was full of black and white pictures of naked ladies. This being the 1940s, the really naughty bits were airbrushed out, but the photos still merited closer inspection! One day I was packed off to a Miss Crouch in Harcourt Road for piano lessons, but did not get on with the lady (whom I regarded as a boring old trout) and subsequently did not turn out to be an Ashkenazi or a Barenboim. (She must have been a good teacher, though—apparently one of her pupils was so talented he could play Chopin's minute waltz in 53 seconds).

When I was five, I started at Rhodes Avenue School, (situated, astonishingly, in Rhodes Avenue) and was there for six happy years. I made friends with Terry, who lived at 86 Victoria Road with his parents, younger sister Carol and older brother Ken, and I stayed friends with the brothers for many years. It was at this school that I first met Miss Perfect, a teacher whom I was to meet again later in life. Already, my sight was diagnosed as not too good, and I recall having drops and being tested for a pair of National Health glasses.

In or around 1945, my parents decided to have me circumcised, presumably for health reasons. (Funny, I didn't look Jewish). In June1946, my sister Kay was born, and in 1948, Mum, Dad and Grandma took me on my first foreign holiday. We went to Victoria Station and caught 'Le Fleche D'Or' (The Golden Arrow Train) which took us down to Toulon. From there we caught another train to Sanary, a delightful town near Bandol on the coast in the south of France. The sun was shining all the time and the glorious white sand was warm under my feet. Bliss!

Strangely, Mum decided to leave the two year old Kay at home, to be looked after by a friend of Mum's called Mrs. Sparks. She was the wife of Chief Superintendent Bert Sparks of the Flying Squad, a formidable man of six foot five, with shoulders and feet to match. He became famous for putting away Alfie Hinds, the career criminal with an IQ of 150.

The next memorable holiday was in 1950, when I was taken to the White Eagle Holiday Camp on Barry Island. This was my first holiday away from my parents, and I had a ball. All the boys were taught to drive a tractor and we all led the outdoor life to the full. On the last day I was presented with a plaster Indian head as a prize for being a 'good boy'—generally thought by the others as a euphemism for 'creep'. We also had family holidays in Reculver and Jaywick: at Jaywick, Kay and I were investigating the house we had rented, when Kay managed (with my help, so she remembers) to go flying out of a fire door, to land bruised and bloodied on the grass six feet below.

In my last year at Rhodes Avenue I wrote, produced, directed and starred in a tribute to the Festival of Britain. This was an exhibition held on the South Bank, which tried to convince the postwar British, at a time when potatoes and (more worryingly) sweets, were still rationed, that better times were just round the corner. My tribute show, entitled, somewhat unimaginatively, 'The Festival of Britain', ended as follows:

Companion: "What was that rollercoaster ride like?"
Me: (looking pale and shaken) "Very scary, but I'm going up again"
Companion: (aghast) "What on earth for?"
Me: "I think I left my stomach up there!" Boom boom!—well, I was only eleven.

Chapter Two

I had done well in the eleven plus exams and was therefore despatched to my parents' first choice of school, Tottenham Grammar School for Boys. Getting there involved a five minute walk to the bus stop, then a twenty minute bus ride to White Hart Lane. On arrival there, all the new boys were given a test to ascertain which stream they would be allocated to; A was good, B was fairly good, C was not very good, D was for the slow ones, and E (no, not what you are thinking) was for Express, to house and fast track the bright ones. I was placed in this E stream, which meant that we would be doing five years' work in four years, and taking our GCEs at fifteen. This was when I started to learn Latin: I was fairly good at languages, and found that Latin helped with my English and French. Not so good was Ken, the boy who sat next to me—his Latin was so bad he didn't even know that Caesar had some jam for tea, and his

French was so bad that he had no idea that his aunt's pen was in his uncle's garden! Because of my National Health glasses and the fact that I was studious rather than sporty, I became known as 'The Professor'. The sports that were played at the school were tennis and rugby, but not football, which was a bit strange for a school situated in White Hart Lane!

I was given my first bike in May, but I had been made to wait quite a while for it, because I (or was it Giggygog?) had accidentally smashed the rear window of a neighbour's car whilst playing cricket in the street. As a punishment, Dad made me wait an extra three months for the bike to be delivered.

It was around this time that Dad took me to Harringay (now spelt Haringey) Stadium to watch the speedway racing. I found it wonderfully exciting, and enjoyed the spectacle, the noise and the smell of the fuel, and we continued to go regularly on a Friday evening. Split Waterman and Ken le Breton (he of the long white scarf) were the two names I remember, and they soon became my heroes. After a while, with the onset of television, attendances dropped, and before long the racing stopped. As I had enjoyed the racing so much, I invented a game of table speedway. This involved setting up an oval track on the table in the sitting room, and using different coloured bottle tops as motor bikes; they would be propelled round the track by striking them with a ruler, and I became very proficient at putting a spin on them, so they would not only move forward from the start line but would also curve round the first bend. Friends would come and play, but I became too good and rarely lost a race. It was the epitome of low-tech, but gave me hours of pleasure. I also started to get hooked on Saturday morning pictures at the Odeon, Muswell Hill, and would thoroughly enjoy the cartoons, the adventure films and the daring escapades of Secret Agent X9.

When I was fifteen, we took our 'O' levels, and I passed in English Language, English Literature, French, Latin and Art, failing in Maths and Chemistry. My parents fully expected me to stay on and take my 'A' levels and subsequently go to university, but I had other ideas—I wanted to get out into the big, wide world. Dad, who was spending a lot of time abroad, was in Persia (as it was then) and was horrified to discover, on his return, that I had left school. I had, however, developed an interest in drawing and painting, and enrolled for Saturday morning classes at the Hornsey School of Art. Unfortunately, I had a short attention span, and left after three or four months. (I later discovered that life drawing classes started the week after I left—what awful timing!).

I soon found a job in the City, paying £4 per week, with Goulandris Bros., a firm of Greek shipowners, whose offices were in St. Mary Axe (right next to where The Gherkin now stands). The old man was Basil Goulandris, and his two sons were John and Dino. Mr. Cooper was the office manager, Grace and Josie were two very attractive secretaries, Molly was the desperately unattractive telephonist from Hull, (or should that be Hell?) and Ernest (Mr. Dino's chauffeur) and Bob (Mr. John's chauffeur) and last, but not least, 'Nobby' Clarke the commissionaire, all of five foot two (which was also his waist measurement), resplendent in his uniform, happy in his authority.

One day, I asked Grace if she would like to go out for a coffee; she agreed, and we arranged to meet that evening. However, on my way down to Bounds Green tube, I had a sudden desire to have another look at a car I had seen and admired the previous day. I had been fascinated by cars for a while now, and coming once again upon this rakish convertible, I had an overwhelming urge to push it out of its open garage and sit in the driver's seat. I reached inside, released the handbrake, and rolled the car gently backwards down the hill, walking alongside the car and steering with my left hand. Unfortunately, (but hardly surprisingly) the car gathered speed and veered over to the left, trapping me against the wall. I tried to pull my leg away and then tried to walk, and promptly fell flat on my face, with my right leg now a funny shape. I cried out 'Help! Help!' and eventually someone heard me, took one look at my leg, and rushed off to call an ambulance. Soon after, I was whisked off to the North Middlesex hospital in Edmonton.

When I awoke next morning, it was to find myself in bed with a metal pin through my right leg just below the knee, attached by rope to a pulley, stretched over a cage over the bed, with a weight on the end. I later discovered that I had fractured my femur, and that by trying to walk I had shortened my leg by three inches; I now had traction to look forward to for at least six weeks.

Visiting by my parents was no easy matter; it involved a round trip of around an hour and a half by public transport to visit their idiot son who had refused to continue his education in order to start work as an office boy with no foreseeable prospects, and was now in hospital as a result of (as they saw it) trying to steal a car. The police called to interview me, and I think I managed to convince them that my actions had resulted from a fascination with cars rather than a desire to steal. The owner of the car felt I had suffered enough, and decided to take no further action.

Hospital life continued in its own unhurried way; patients arrived and patients left, nurses and doctors visited regularly, as did a formidable matron (whatever happened to matrons?) and physiotherapy consisted of a tall, slim attractive lady stroking my upper leg while we did a crossword together. One day I wrote to the Daily Express to offer my views on the establishment's unfavourable reaction to the news that Princess Margaret wanted to marry Group Captain Peter Townsend, a divorcee. They sent me a telegram saying 'MAY WE HAVE PERMISSION PRINT POINTS FROM YOUR LETTER' I sent them a telegram saying 'YES' (monosyllabic, that's me), and that was the end of it, the letter never was printed—they must have thought my views too controversial to print.

Now and again friends visited; Terry, who had gone on to Trinity School from Rhodes Avenue, called more than once, and sometimes dragged sundry mates along with him. One evening, Grace and Josie from the office came to pay me a visit and my stock on the ward went up enormously, having two such glamorous ladies at my bedside, and Grace very graciously (how else?) forgave me for standing her up. Eventually, after about three months, I was discharged, but had to use crutches for three weeks, and soon after that I returned to work. On my seventeenth birthday, Dad bought his first car—a blue and cream Ford Zephyr, with a three speed gearbox and the gear lever on the steering column. Terry's father was a long distance lorry driver and agreed to give me driving lessons—I had many lessons with him, and one with Thames Valley School of Motoring, and passed my test first time. I asked Dad if I could borrow the car the following Saturday evening to celebrate, and drove off down the A127 towards Southend. Whilst overtaking a line of slower cars, the heavens opened and I got into a skid. More by luck than judgement, I managed to control the car, but decided to cut my journey short and return home, suitably chastened. I realised that a slightly lower powered car would be better for me, so I asked Mr. Dino if the company would lend me £25 to buy a car (a Hillman 6). He looked flabbergasted that anyone could buy a car for £25 (what with he and his brother having chauffeur-driven Bentleys), but he agreed.

Terry and I had met two sisters who lived in Brighton, and two or three times we drove down to the coast to see them in the afore-mentioned Hillman. One evening, I was driving us back past the two enormous black cats cast in bronze outside the Carreras cigarette building in Mornington Crescent and started to doze off at the wheel. Only Terry's alertness saved us from at best an accident, or at worst, killing us.

I realised that I was getting nowhere at Goulandris Bros. and gave in my notice, only to start work the following month as a petrol pump attendant at Thirlestane Garage, in Colney Hatch Lane (a real career advancement!).

Later that year, having disposed of the Hillman, I bought an ex-London Vintage taxi. It was cavernous inside and often half a dozen of us would get together for a party in the back. One day, the throttle linkage broke, and I asked a new friend, Timmy, if he could do anything for me. He worked under the bonnet for half an hour and declared the problem solved. He, Terry's brother Ken and I set off to do a road test; Ken decided he wanted a better view of the surroundings and clambered up onto the roof, so we set off from outside Rockville with me driving, Timmy in the back and Ken up above. I immediately realised that Timmy had replaced the throttle linkage the wrong way round; when I put my foot down, the revs almost died to a tickover and when I took my foot off the throttle the revs increased. The method of driving was now to put the clutch and throttle to the floor and then lift both feet simultaneously, repeating the manoeuvre whenever a gearchange was required. This meant that I didn't need either foot to propel the vehicle, in fact I could stand on the running board, waving arms and legs at bewildered passers by. I called to Timmy in the back and asked him to take over the driving, and then clambered onto the bonnet and then up on to the roof to join a startled Ken.

The taxi gave us enormous fun, and we would often drive down to Brighton, and, if we felt really adventurous, further afield to Margate. Nearer to home, Ken and I had a sudden desire to test the taxi's aquatic ability, and one afternoon drove serenely through the pond on top of Hampstead Heath. The taxi passed this test with flying colours.

Lonnie Donegan was very popular at the time with his very catchy skiffle music, so Terry, Alan (Terry was going out with Alan's younger sister Janet) and I decided to form a skiffle group. Alan (the only one with any musical ability) played the guitar, Terry played the bass (a tea chest with a bit of string attached to a pole sticking out of one of the corners) and I played the washboard. Our playing was appalling and was surpassed in tunelessness only by our singing, which was even worse. Consequently, we did not survive for very long, and thoughts of living the pop star life were quickly shattered. One evening, however, while driving through Hampstead to or from one of our rare gigs, an amazing coincidence occurred; we spotted another ex-London vintage taxi, the driver was called Tony and he was a member of a skiffle group—how weird was that?

In June, I went to the Odeon in Muswell Hill to see 'The Girl Can't Help It', a rock and roll musical film starring Eddie Cochran, Gene Vincent, Fats Domino and a staggeringly pneumatic Jayne Mansfield. The scene where the milkman's glasses shatter when he first catches sight of her has stayed in my memory for ever, as has Eddie Cochran's first appearance, which was greeted with delighted screams from the teeny boppers who thought he was Elvis.

In July 1957 a baby girl called Angela Nerena was born in Epsom—but more of her later, seventeen years later.

Terry had made friends with a boy called Bruce at Trinity School. He lived in Durnsford Road, opposite the swimming pool (it's now a garden centre), next door to two teenage sisters called Jill and Sue, and he assured us that if we hid behind one of the pillars in the car park next to the swimming pool and stood on tiptoe, we would be able to see Jill getting undressed for bed. This seemed an excellent idea to us and we watched spellbound one evening as Jill displayed her magnificent charms. We later got introduced to them both (the sisters, not Jill's charms) on a slightly more formal basis, and Terry ended up marrying Sue. Their father was outwardly a stern character who ran a successful car hire business, but underneath his slightly forbidding exterior he was quite friendly. As a teenager, he had lost a leg in a motorcycle accident and he now sported a screw-on wooden leg. It was he who gave me a salutary lesson in the art of being towed. A crowd of us had gone to Richmond Park in a couple of cars, one of which was Dad's Zephyr, and it broke down. Jill, who was with me, said 'Don't worry, I'll get my father to come and sort it out.' Her father duly arrived three quarters of an hour later looking understandably peeved, and decided that he couldn't repair it on the spot, but agreed to tow me home. He attached the towrope to his car and Dad's Zephyr and off we went. This turned out to be the most frightening drive imaginable. In my opinion, he was driving far too fast, and on numerous occasions I nearly drove into the back of him. We eventually got home with me a quivering wreck, then, to my astonishment, he got out of his car, incandescent with rage and shouted 'You bloody fool, don't you know that you have to do the braking for both of us?' I pointed out that it was the first time I had ever been towed and, no, I didn't know that I should have been braking for both of us. We both learnt a lesson that day, but luckily both cars survived unscathed.

In February, the plane carrying the Manchester United football team back from Munich crashed on take off, killing many of the team. Bobby Charlton was one of the few survivors.

In November 1958, an eighteen year old Cliff Richard burst on to the pop scene with his first record 'Move It'—it was the B side of the record, but the one that all the teenagers loved. In July 1959 he appeared in his first film (in which he played a young thug!) which was called 'Serious Charge' and it gave him his first no.1, Livin' Doll. It was a very catchy record, but after six weeks at no. 1, most people (including me) were heartily sick of it.

Later that year I was getting restless at Thirlestane Garage. I didn't particularly like the owner, Mr. Gelber, nor his Sales Manager, Mr. Digby. Mr. Gelber was a tall, bald, arrogant man, and Mr. Digby was short and plump, with delicate, baby-like pink skin and a pipe which was rarely removed from his mouth. I realised that I was getting nowhere fast; serving petrol, selling accessories and moving Renault Dauphines from one side of the forecourt to the other were beginning to lose their allure. Then, one day, a van with the legend 'Crimpy Crisps' written all over it pulled in for petrol, and I got chatting to the driver. It transpired that the company were looking for a van salesman to sell their crisps to pubs, restaurants, off licences, etc. I applied to their Head Office in March (that's a place, not the month) and was duly interviewed and offered a job covering Greater London, Surrey and what was then Middlesex. Having given in my notice at the garage, I started work as a van salesman on 17th. August 1959. I enjoyed the job on quite a few levels; I loved the driving and the freedom and I discovered that I was quite good at selling. In November, the country's first motorway, the M1, was opened, and in December,

I was asked to go to March for a sales conference. It was just before Christmas, and the weather was very cold.

I set off in the morning and was driving up through Berkshire on very quiet roads, when the car in front of me suddenly braked for no apparent reason. I soon realised why when I went into a gentle pirouette on the ice and slid off the road backwards down a slope, coming to rest against a wire fence. Again, luckily, neither I nor the van had been damaged, and in due course, after I had been towed out, (I did the braking for both of us!) I continued the journey.

We had the conference the next day, and I came out from various tests and questionnaires with flying colours and high praise from the senior management.

Chapter Three

I spent Christmas at home with the family, and all of a sudden it was the beginning of the sixties. They did not start promisingly for me. I went to work on Monday 3rd January in the pouring rain and got soaked. I put the heater in the van on full blast and continued my round. The following day I woke up with a nasty cold but did a day's work anyway. By Wednesday it had developed into the flu, and I phoned in sick. By the Sunday, I had become delirious and was rushed off to Hornsey General Hospital where they diagnosed pneumonia. During the week, Terry, Sue and Jill came to visit me, and Terry offered to give me his new jacket that Sue wouldn't let him wear. It appeared to have been made from a material similar to that used to make the fabric of deckchairs. I accepted it, much to Jill's disgust.

On Monday, 24th January (my twentieth birthday), I left hospital, proudly wearing my deckchair jacket. I resumed work on the Wednesday, and received a memo from Head Office that the landlord of the Three Pigeons pub in Richmond wanted to see me. When I got there, he presented me with a packet of crisps that a customer had returned to him. I emptied the contents onto the counter, and out fell a dead rat. I explained to him that it was a new flavour we were experimenting with, and I would be delighted to hear his reaction. His reaction was to explain, in graphic detail, what I could do with the rat and my order book and my van and various other sundry objects. It was about then that I realised that abject, grovelling apologies were more what he was looking for and that is what I offered. I wrote a memo to Head Office telling them the story, and they sent him a case of crisps and a bottle of wine. We held on to the account and the landlord forgave us. In the twenty first century, litigation and thousands of pounds in compensation would have been the order of the day.

On 2nd February a twenty two year old Buddy Holly died in a plane crash—his death would later be referred to as 'the day the music died' in Don McClean's record 'American Pie'.

Later that month, delivering to a shop in Harrow, I saw the most beautiful young blonde girl behind the counter of the chemist shop next door. She was busy serving, so I couldn't stop and chat. However, when I got home that evening, I composed a letter telling her that I thought she was beautiful, and would she like to go out with me. In April, I received a letter from a young lady called Carol, who worked in the chemist shop in Harrow. Because I had not known her name, nor the exact address, my letter had taken seven weeks to reach her. However, it was worth the wait, because we embarked on a very pleasant relationship for several months. (A thought—if I had successfully chatted up a girl in a shop selling Wedgwood, Minton and Crown Derby, would that have constituted a pull in a china shop?)

On 17th April twenty one year old Eddie Cochran died in a car crash during his tour of Great Britain. Vince Eager was among the mourners at his funeral.

By July, I was beginning to get itchy feet again and started looking for interesting job adverts. I applied to, amongst others, BOAC, BEA (before they amalgamated to become BA) and Key Flats. Key Flats, or the London County Freehold and Leasehold Properties Ltd. to give them their somewhat long-winded official name, offered me an interview and I went to see a Mr. Finch at the Highgate branch. The job entailed working in that particular branch of a large property company, managing blocks of mansion flats in South Close, Muswell Hill Road and Southwood Lane. I was getting disillusioned with Crimpy Crisps because of issues concerning my

Sales Manager. I had a high regard for him, but he told me he was about to be sacked. I told the powers that be that if they sacked him, I would resign. They duly sacked him, and I duly resigned.

Later that month, just to show that they could do it without Cliff, the Shadows were at no. 1 with 'Apache'.

I was now out of work, but heard that British Car Auctions at Alexandra Palace were looking for people to deliver cars sold at auction. I applied, and although the work was very spasmodic, I jumped at the chance to drive various cars. In September, Key Flats wrote to me offering me the job in Highgate, to start on 1st October. In the meantime, I was charging about all over the country delivering cars. It was this temporary job that provided me with a very weird experience. I was asked to deliver a Hillman Minx to Nottingham. I collected the car at nine o'clock in the morning, and set off up the A1. By twelve thirty I began to feel peckish, so I pulled off the main road to find a sandwich shop. I found one, parked the car and crossed the road to resume my journey. It was then that I noticed that the clutch pedal had disappeared. I was completely stunned—I had driven the car for about a hundred miles, changing gear whenever necessary, and now the clutch pedal was no longer there. I sat in the car utterly flabbergasted—what on earth could have happened? I searched the footwell in the vain hope that the pedal had fallen off, but to no avail. I started to think that I was going mad. I got out of the car to clear my head, and it was then that I spotted, immediately behind me, an identical Hillman Minx. I had got into the wrong car, an automatic, which didn't need a clutch pedal. I got back into the correct car, and continued my journey, shaking my head in disbelief at my stupidity.

Later that month Bruce and I went to see Cliff Richard's second film 'Expresso Bongo', which had been written by Wolf Mankowitz and starred Laurence Harvey. Little did we know then that they would both loom large in our lives in years to come.

In October, I started work at Key Flats. Our offices were down half a dozen steps off the Highgate end of the Muswell Hill Road, right opposite a bus stop (of which more later). The staff comprised the manager, Mr. Finch, a short, fat, bald man with a propensity for swearing, his secretary, Wendy, his assistant (me), the clerk of works, Alan, and various porters, all resplendent (just like Nobby Clarke at Goulandris Bros) in their uniforms, and two workmen, Jack and Jim. These two looked like stock characters in a comedy about the building trade (think Andy Capp, the cartoon character in the Daily Mirror). Jack was about six foot three, with overalls and a flat cap which never left his head, and Jim, who was about five foot two, with overalls and a flat cap which never left his head. The irony was that Jim, the short one, was the boss, because Jack, the tall one, was a bit thick. They were responsible for any repairs and maintenance to the property, and reported directly to the clerk of works. He and his wife Judy lived in a nice flat at the top of Southwood Lane. I would, in time, get to know this flat quite well.

I was now seeing Jill on a regular basis; she was a very pretty plump girl with a bubbly personality, but there was no sexual spark between us; however, we spent many a happy evening together with Terry and Sue. I then met a lovely girl called Diane, who, discovering that I liked classical music, took me to the last night of the proms. Our romance didn't last for very long though—she was swept off her feet by a young pop star called Vince Eager (he was one of the stable run by Larry Parnes, the impresario, who gave his lads what I regarded as somewhat silly names: Billy Fury, Adam Faith, Tommy Steele, Marty Wilde, Dickie Pride, Johnny Gentle etc.) In the face of such competition, such nomenclature, what chance did I, a mere Shelton, stand?

Early in 1961 I met a girl called Viv, who lived just around the corner in Clifton Road. She, an attractive, smartly dressed girl and I became firm friends and, showing early signs of an entrepreneurial spirit, we placed an advert in the local paper, something along the lines of 'Group of local youngsters seek work—anything legal considered'. We were delighted to receive a reply from the actor, Michael Hordern, who was looking for part-time gardening help. Terry, Sue, Ken, Viv and I all trooped along to his house in Highgate, and were given instructions as to what we were required to do. We laboured away for a couple of hours, and, when we had finished, discovered that Michael Hordern had departed, but we had been left a very decent tea and £1 ten shillings. We felt this to be overly generous, and left the ten shilling note. No further replies were received, and none of us had green fingers, so the whole thing fizzled out.

In April, the E Type Jaguar was launched at the Geneva Motor Show, to worldwide astonishment and acclaim. Indeed, Enzo Ferrari, who presumably knew about these things, pronounced it to be the most beautiful car in the world. Later that month, Bruce and I went to see Cliff's third film 'The Young Ones', the title song from which entered the charts at no.1.

Bruce had now got himself a job as a hairdresser on board a cruise ship, and was having a great time travelling the world, and seducing as many of his clients as he could cope with. Jill was working as a nurse and, towards the end of the year, got a job and a flat in Wanstead. Terry was working for Jill and Sue's dad at the car hire company, which he would one day be in charge of. In

September, the Shadows were again at no. 1, this time with 'Kon-Tiki'.

Early in 1962, I answered an advert in the local paper. The Brevis Amateur Film Unit were looking for budding young actors and actresses to appear in a film called 'Welcome to Citizenship', which was to be about young people coming of age in the borough. Bruce had now returned from his travels, and was going out with a young Jewish beauty queen who was the current Miss Wood Green (whom, for some reason that now eludes me, I christened 'Miss Plastic Dustbins') and he, his girlfriend, various others and I all went along to the auditions in Wood Green. She and I both got cast, and spent many a happy evening rehearsing and filming.

In March, I got up one morning to find Grandma dead on the toilet. She had apparently got up in the middle of the night and suffered a heart attack. I called down to Mum and together we put her back to bed and phoned Dad, who immediately came back from work and made all the necessary funeral arrangements. I was very sorry to lose her, because she had had a big influence in my upbringing. With Mum working for the North Thames Gas Board and Dad spending a lot of time abroad on business, she was often the one I had turned to when younger. It was she who had saved a young friend's life years earlier: he was choking on a boiled sweet, and she picked him up by his ankles, upended him, and shook him until the sweet fell out. It was also she who came up with the finest put down I have ever heard. We were having tea one day with Mum, Dad, Grandma, Mum's brother Harry and his wife and son, and Kay and me. We were all seated round the tea table and there was a constant babble of noise, most of it coming from Uncle Harry. All of a sudden, there was a lull in the conversation, and Uncle Harry turned to Dad and said 'You don't say much, do you, Ernie?' Before my father had a chance to reply, Grandma said 'No—he usually waits until he has something worthwhile to say'.

Later that month, a crowd of us went to see Johnny Kidd and the Pirates at Hornsey Town Hall, and I was seeing a girl called Alice (I never did get her into Wonderland, though). She was good fun, but a bit thick. I asked her one evening if she thought we should join the Common Market. 'Do what?' came the baffled reply.

In August, Marilyn Monroe was found dead in bed, aged thirty six, and, to this day, no-one is certain how she died. Dad and I had been to see her in 'Some Like it Hot', with Jack Lemmon and Tony Curtis. Her acting was nothing special, but, oh boy, could she light up the screen.

Bruce and I would often go to El Toro, a restaurant in Muswell Hill, for a Spaghetti Bolognese, and it was there that I first spotted Julie, one of the waitresses She was a big girl—tall, red headed, with a great figure that was best appreciated as she leant over to put our plates on the table. Jill (having moved back from Wanstead) announced that as her parents were away, she was having a party at their house so I invited big Julie. The party was terrific, with lots of drink and loud music. Eventually, things quietened down, and guests either left or found a place to sleep. Julie and I bagged the downstairs sofa bed, and things were just beginning to get interesting when Julie staggered out of bed to be sick (Tony Shelton—the Great Lover!) When she returned, both of us had lost interest and went to sleep.

Kay had a friend called Lesley who used to come round to Rockville, and one evening, when Kay went to bed, Lesley didn't get up to leave, but stayed chatting with me and made it obvious that she was interested. I was flattered that such a pretty, precocious teenager found me attractive and I started an affair with her that would last for years.

In April a crowd of us went to see Morecambe and Wise at the Wood Green Theatre (this was before they made it big on television, but it was obvious from their act that they would make it big before too long) and one day, Kay came home with her Religious Instruction teacher, a very pretty Welsh redhead. She and I immediately hit it off, she not ramming religion down my throat, and me not telling her that I was an agnostic, going on atheist. We had a good fling, but in August I was once again with Alice as a crowd of us drove down to Clacton to celebrate Bruce's 21st birthday. We had a barbecue on the beach, and later I tried, unsuccessfully, to make love to Alice on the back seat of Dad's Zodiac. (I never did convince him to get a stretch limo). Christmas was again spent at home with the family.

Chapter Four

Early in 1963, Viv, Mark, his wife Christine and I decided to start going to Civil Defence classes in Wood Green (whose idea was that?)—but it didn't catch on, and we stopped going as quickly as we had started. In February, Viv got to hear of a new restaurant and she, John, Terry and Sue, Jill and I went out for the evening to the Bridge House in Reigate. How strange that over thirty years later I would be living in a house not half a mile away. We wined and dined and were serenaded by a very pathetic violinist, and we all felt terribly grand. (My apologies—that was a typing error in the previous sentence—it should have read 'serenaded by a peripatetic violinist').

By now, the Beatles had started their domination of the charts. Their first record, 'Love Me Do', released in October 1962, only got to no. 17, but their next five releases, 'Please Please Me', 'From Me To You', 'She

Loves You', 'I Want To Hold Your Hand' and 'Can't Buy Me Love' were all smash hits, 'Please Please Me' being the only one not to get to no.1 (it merely got to no. 2).

My eyesight, though not deteriorating, was not improving either, so I figured if you can't ignore it, make the best of it. Two of the pop stars of the day were Buddy Holly, sadly now deceased, and Hank Marvin of the Shadows, both of whom wore black horn rimmed glasses. I beetled round to my local optician and ordered a pair. The following week, Bruce and I (magnificently sporting my new horn rims) were having a coffee in El Toro; if Bruce had entered a Cliff Richard Lookalike Competition, he would have won and Cliff would have come a poor second. We noticed a couple of girls at a nearby table, whispering and casting furtive glances in our direction.

Eventually, they plucked up courage and came over to our table. 'Could we have your autographs please?' (Ah, the joy of specs.)

In March, I was called to deal with a problem in a flat in South Close, and the door was opened by a delightful Spanish girl called Mercedes, who was the au-pair. I sorted the problem out, and asked Mercedes out for a drink the following evening. I told Dad I wanted to impress her and could I borrow the Zodiac?

(Did I tell you that I now owned the Zephyr and he had bought a Zodiac?) He reluctantly agreed, and I drove up to South Close to collect her; she jumped in, and we set off towards the traffic lights at the end of Muswell Hill Road; as I swing round to the right, Mercedes slid gracefully along the bench seat and fell out of the door that she hadn't closed properly. This was in the days when front bench seats were the norm, and safety belts hadn't been thought of. I screeched to a halt, leapt out, picked her up and put her back in the car, and locked the passenger door.

'Did you hurt yourself?' I asked, pleased beyond belief that she hadn't been run over by a bus. 'I think I have the bruise on my thigh' she exclaimed in her halting English. I drove on for a while until I found a nice secluded spot, and spent a delightful half hour inspecting her bruise from as many angles as possible.

I regularly bought the New Musical Express to keep up with the latest news about the pop music scene, and to see how the Beatles and Cliff and the Shadows were doing in the charts, and in one issue they announced that they were looking for junior reporters; they asked interested applicants to send in an article about a pop star and the best article would win the author a job at the NME. I knew (but I can't remember how I knew) that Cliff and his family lived in Percy Road, Winchmore Hill, so one evening I drove there to see if could get an interview. I knocked on the door, which was answered by his sister Donna, who announced that he was out. I chatted to her for a while and then Cliff and his mother rolled up in a black Ford Thunderbird. It was obvious that he didn't have any time to spare, so I drove home and wrote an article about our fleeting meeting (nice little rhyme there)—it was headed 'Cliff's Going Down—Under' (a reference to his impending trip to Australia). I received a very complimentary letter back, but was not offered the job.

Later that month, a crowd of us went to see Cliff and the Shadows at the Finsbury Park Astoria, where it was confirmed by all and sundry that Bruce did indeed look more like Cliff than Cliff did. (I just kept quiet and admired Hank's glasses).

In August, I met a girl called Deidre De'ath, who suffered permanently from jokes about her looking like De'ath warmed up—it didn't take me too long to realise that the jokes were not entirely without foundation, and as far as our relationship was concerned, this turned out to be the kiss of De'ath.

In October, after a lot of hard work, 'Welcome to Citizenship' was at last completed, and given its premiere at Wood Green Town Hall. I was a film star! There was a good turnout of friends, family, the Mayor, councillors and everybody who had had anything at all to do with the production, and the film was generally well received. (I managed to get hold of a copy over forty years later, and cringed with embarrassment at the production, direction, acting, and, worst of all, what a prat I looked. (Film star? Hah!)

Bruce and I regularly used to ask John out in the evenings on our eternal quest to find new girls, but he was much more interested in amateur dramatics, and was always rehearsing. He belonged to the St. Saviours Amateur Dramatic Society in Alexandra Park Road and in early November invited me to go along and see a show he was in. ('Milestones', seeing as you ask) I did so, thoroughly enjoyed the evening, and decided to join the group. It was then that I met Miss Perfect again or, as she had now become, Mrs. Freda Rayner. She had married a chap called Stuart Rayner, who, although not the tiniest man I had ever met, was certainly on the short list. I successfully auditioned for the part of the doctor in 'Blithe Spirit', by Noel Coward, we started rehearsals the following week, and my career in the amateur theatre was underway.

Since Grandma died, the upstairs of Rockville had been empty, so Dad decided to let it out, and had placed an advert in the local paper. A week later, we had a reply from a young lady called Anne, who was interested in taking the flat. She came to see it and agreed terms, and it was arranged that I would collect her and her belongings from Streatham on 22nd November in the Zodiac. We were driving back during the evening when a news flash came on the radio—President John F. Kennedy had been assassinated in Dallas. He had been a charismatic president, and I felt a sense of personal loss, and it was two very subdued people who arrived back at Rockville late that evening. Anne settled in nicely, stayed for almost a year, and went out with John for a while.

As a Christmas treat, we booked tickets for a show at the Finsbury Park Astoria, and on Christmas Eve, Bruce, his current girlfriend, Terry, Sue, Jill and I went to see Billy J. Kramer and the Dakotas, Cilla Black and the Beatles. From the moment the Beatles arrived on stage to the moment they left it, every note sung and chord played was drowned by the girls in the audience who screamed at the top of their voices, and we didn't really get to hear what the hell they were playing. But we were all able to say we saw the Beatles live on stage.

Chapter Five

All of a sudden, it was another year, and the sixties were now getting into their stride. England in general and London in particular had become the focal point for all that was cool; along with the Beatles and Cliff, The Stones, The Kinks, The Who, Terence Stamp, Julie Christie, Twiggy, Jean Shrimpton, the E Type Jaguar, the Mini and the mini-skirt were all weaving their magic around the world. Although the pill would not be made available to single girls until 1967, these very same girls were embracing (or practising for) their new-found sexual freedom with open arms (and legs), and it was all systems go. From the mystery of suspender belts and stocking tops, hidden under petticoats, it was suddenly the 'in your face' of mini skirts But I would not, dear reader, want you to think that it was just about girls—perish the thought. I had now taken up painting but discovered, to my immense frustration, that my paintings didn't look anything like what had been intended; portraits, landscapes, seascapes, they were all unrecognisable. It was this that made me try abstracts—if the finished article didn't look like anything, then what did it matter? Dad took a look at one such effort and offered to buy it. This astonished me, and persuaded me that I might have some talent after all, and I produced many more abstracts during the following months. I was also getting more and more involved with the amateur theatre, both acting and designing programme covers and was still mad about cars, dividing my time between driving the Zephyr, the Zodiac, and the Key Flats minivan. Alan and his wife Judy were now proud parents and were asking me to babysit regularly, and it was often arranged that I would take the van home after work, collect whichever young lady was to be my guest for the evening, spend the evening at the flat, drive her home later, keep the van overnight and drive to work in it the following morning. Mr. Finch would probably not have approved, but, luckily, he never got to know. Had he done so I would, no doubt, have been regaled with one of his diatribes, and told that I was not fit to be a pox doctor's clerk!

It was around this time that I made a note of the number of the telephone box by the bus stop, immediately opposite the office on the other side of the road. One evening, after the usual evening queue had developed, I rang the number. The girl at the head of the queue answered it, and I asked her if it was cold waiting for the bus, and wasn't it lucky that she had such a lovely green coat to keep her warm. She looked around in order to discover who she was talking to, not realising that it was me, hiding in my darkened office. She eventually put the phone down in bewilderment, and, after she had got on her bus, I repeated the process with whoever was the new head of the queue. This gave me and the girls in the office hours of fun.

John, who suffered from epilepsy, and who had been instrumental in my getting involved with the amateur theatre, was getting increasingly frustrated with his employer's intransigent attitude to his shift work requirements, and started looking elsewhere. The Wills tobacco company invited him down to Bristol for an interview and subsequently offered him a job. He moved to Bristol in January, and soon met Sandra, who was later to become his wife.

It was about this time that I started a car cleaning round. There was a classy block of flats called Whitehall Lodge in Muswell Hill Road, and I decided to canvass there one Saturday morning, and immediately found two residents who would be delighted to have their cars cleaned on a regular basis. It developed over the months into quite a lucrative business, and had the added bonus of my being involved with various cars.

I was still seeing Kay's friend Lesley, albeit somewhat irregularly, and was still seeing Jill, Sue and Terry most weeks. I was also spending an increasing amount of time rehearsing, and we performed 'Blithe Spirit' in April, and I was suddenly hooked on the live theatre. Filming was all very well, but it never involved audience reaction, and I felt most at home when I could interact with, and have some control over, a live audience. However, the Brevis Amateur Film Unit contacted me to ask if I would be interested in appearing in their next film, to be called 'A Young Man's Fancy', with me and a very attractive young lady called Jean playing the only two parts. I jumped at the chance—I thoroughly enjoyed acting in front of the camera, audience or no audience, and so we started shooting the following Sunday morning in Finsbury Park. I was told to report at 10 o'clock in a smart suit, and within minutes of starting shooting, a young lad came up to me and said 'Cor, mister, you doin' an advert for Burtons? (I took this to be a compliment on my impeccable dress sense). We later repaired to somebody's flat to film 'the seduction scene', which involved Jean and I taking off most of our clothes and getting on a bed. Jean had been told in advance about what was required and had promptly gone out and bought a new set of lacy green underwear. I, unaware of the demands of the scene, was mortified to be revealed in a vest and pants that didn't match and had seen better days. However, the film was completed within two weeks and shown at Wood Green

Town Hall in March. I have no recollection of how it was received or what filmgoers thought of my underwear.

At St. Saviours we started rehearsals for 'Dry Rot', the very popular Whitehall farce, and I auditioned for, and was cast in, the Brian Rix part. Due to unprecedented public demand (?) 'Welcome to Citizenship' had its second showing at Wood Green Town Hall on 18th March, and on 30th March a crowd of us went to see Cliff and the Shadows at the Finsbury Park Astoria (loved the glasses, Hank).

In April, we performed 'Dry Rot' at St. Saviours, which was a rip-roaring success, and I learnt how intoxicating it could be to have an audience in stitches. Later that month, the Brevis AFU were again in touch about their next film, 'Soliloquy', this time with me as the sole actor; however, I won't bore you with the details because I can't remember them.

In May, Bruce left for Clacton to become a Butlin's Redcoat, and I got to know a guy called Graham and his girlfriend Melanie, and in July he invited me to go on holiday with him to Devon and Cornwall in his Fiat 500. It was not a great success—Graham and I were both over 6ft. tall, and the Fiat was the smallest car I had ever been in, and it had the dubious distinction of being the slowest car from rest to 60 mph ever tested by Autocar magazine. The upside of all this was that I got very friendly with Melanie on our return.

With Mum and Grandma in the
South of France.

Outside Rockville with
sister Kay.

The debonair taxi driver and his motley crew.

Carol from the chemist's shop, who
eventually answered my letter.

Eager to give me the elbow – Diane,
who left me for a pop star.

Proudly sporting my Hank Marvin glasses, rehearsing for 'Welcome to Citizenship' with Miss Plastic Dustbins.

With friends and family around the much loved Zephyr.

At a party with Graham, desperately trying to look cool.

On 12th June, Nelson Mandela was convicted of plotting to overthrow the government, jailed for life and sent to Robben Island.

In August we again went to see the Beatles at the Finsbury Park Odeon, and on 27th the lads went down to Clacton to meet up with Bruce to celebrate Terry's stag night. This was, very wisely, held two days before his wedding to Sue, so we all had time to recover from the festivities. The wedding was at St. Saviours on the Saturday, with his brother Ken as best man. As Bruce and I were striding up Alexandra Park Road in our sharp new suits, a photographer leapt out and took a load of photos of us, only to curse us later when he realised that we were not the groom and best man! We all retired to the Cock pub for the wedding breakfast, and then on to 135 Durnsford Road for the evening.

I had met a girl called Mary through the drama group, and was now seeing her regularly; she was plump and had a lovely sense of humour, and we did a number of plays together. In September Bruce returned from Clacton exhausted, having given his all in providing a holiday to remember for hundreds of young ladies.

Terry and Sue had now got on to the property ladder by buying a house in Enfield, and a crowd of us were invited to a party to celebrate. Jill and I arrived just after lunchtime, and I spent the greater part of the afternoon frolicking in their pool. The sun was shining and the booze was flowing, and after a while, I crashed out on a bed, wearing only my swimming trunks and a silly smile. When I awoke, I discovered that my trunks had been removed, and had been replaced by a daffodil, gently nestling between my buttocks. Jill's Mum then berated me for leaving lipstick stains all over the sheets! All very strange—and me fast asleep!

I was now completely immersed in the amateur drama scene, learning about all aspects of putting on a play; rehearsals were taking up quite a bit of time, and energy, as was babysitting for Alan and Judy, but I thoroughly enjoyed both.

Christmas was celebrated with lunch at home, tea at 135 Durnsford Road, and the evening at Bruce's house.

Boxing Day evening found me at 135 again. Snow fell and another year was almost over.

Chapter Six

1965 started with Viv and I vowing to write a farce. While suffering from writers' block one evening (a terrible affliction which was to strike us both down on many an occasion), we spotted an advert in the Evening Standard. A chap called Bill Kendall, of the Overseas Development Office in Whitehall, was proposing to take 'She Stoops to Conquer', a Restoration comedy by Oliver Goldsmith, on a tour of Austria and Germany, and was looking for actors and actresses. Viv and I applied for an audition, and were subsequently cast as servants to Mr. Hardcastle, the master of the house. The tour was scheduled to go later that year, but was eventually postponed until 1966, and we ended up rehearsing for 'She Stoops' and 'The Happiest Days of Your Life' simultaneously.

Bruce, meanwhile, had been looking for a flat to rent, and in January he found one in Mountview Road, Hornsey. He invited me to move in with him, and I did so. He had now met a slightly dodgy character called Ralph, who ran a minicab firm from a sleazy office in Carnaby Street, and was driving for him on a part time basis.

In February, Graham and Melanic got married, and I was working the odd night shift in Carnaby Street. One night, we got a call from a young lady who wanted to be picked up from a Kensington hotel and taken to North Finchley, and I was despatched to collect her. It was about three o'clock in the morning when I got to the hotel, and she came out and slumped into the seat next to me. On the way to her house we got talking, and she told me that she was a nurse, and that the previous day a very prosperous Arab had invited her to his hotel for the evening. She had gone along, and by the time I collected her, she had earned more money for four hours with the Arab than she earned in a month as a nurse. When I dropped her off, she gave me a good tip, and I pondered the effects of oil wealth, NHS funding, and life in general.

In March I attended the Key Flats annual dinner and dance, which was a big do for managerial, clerical and works staff held at Derry and Toms in Kensington. This was memorable for being the first time that I had heard the 'f' word over a loudspeaker system. The managing director, a gentleman rejoicing in the name of R Gordon

Dashwood, gave a speech, culminating in a story about a Key Flats employee who had climbed a ladder without taking the necessary safety precautions, which ended thus: 'and he fell off the ladder, breaking his fucking neck!'

On 27th March Viv's friend Sue married Nick. Nick was a very strange character who dressed from head to toe in black, wore a black stovepipe hat and drove (very dangerously) a Black Humber Hawk. They lived in a flat over Bounds Green tube station with a pet rat called Desdemona. (Takes all sorts).

Later that month, interspersed with rehearsals for 'She Stoops to Conquer', and the new St. Saviours production, 'Tons of Money', Viv and I were still attempting to write a farce, and I was also by now designing and drawing the programme covers for all the St. Saviours shows. Life was hectic, what with numerous girlfriends, rehearsals, and spasmodic stints as a minicab driver in the early hours—but, what the hell, it sure wasn't boring. It was about to get a lot less boring.

In June, Viv spotted an advert (she was a one for adverts, that Viv) in the Barnet Press for people who would be interested in getting involved in a pantomime called 'Beastie and the Beaut', and we made contact with Justin and his wife Michelle; we met them for a drink, and the following week went round to their house in North Finchley. Justin was the spitting image of Manfred

Mann, another bespectacled pop star, and his wife was a very attractive French girl with a sexy accent, a dirty laugh, and an even dirtier mind.

We were to get to know them both very well indeed.

Bruce's younger sister Miriam had by now married a Hell's Angel lookalike called Reg, and in August Jill and I accompanied them to Butlins at Clacton for the day. (I hope we weren't looking for Bruce—he'd left ages ago).

At the end of August I was off on holiday to Tossa de Mar by coach, through France with an overnight stop in Clermont Ferrand. A nice two weeks in the sun, and then it was back to sample Michelle's charms. Viv and I were subsequently invited to Sunday lunch, which took about four hours. We started with soup, then a break for the first bottle of wine and a cigarette (sorry, didn't I tell you I was smoking twenty a day?), then the main course, then a break for another cigarette and to open a second bottle of wine, then cheese and biscuits, followed by more wine and another cigarette, then coffee, brandy and another cigarette. Boy, did we think we were the height of sophistication. All thoughts of producing a pantomime had long since receded, and Justin (resplendent in his Manfred Mann glasses) was making a play (and I'm not talking about for the stage) for Viv.

In October John announced his engagement to Sandra, and Justin, Michelle, Viv and I were invited to a party at Eve and Frank's house. Eve and Frank were friends of John and Michelle, and whereas Michelle was very sexy, Eve was stunningly beautiful, and completely wasted on her husband.

I heard through the Key Flats grapevine that the post of assistant manager at the Baker Street branch had become available, and I went along for an interview. I thought that, for once, this could be a good career move, and was delighted when I heard, two weeks later, that the job was mine if I wanted it.

At the end of October, Viv and I appeared in 'Don't Utter a Note' by Anton Delmar, and early in March, I started work in the West End as the assistant manager to Mr. S. D. Briggs. Our offices were in the basement of Bickenhall Mansions, an island site of large flats bounded by Baker Street, Marylebone Road, Gloucester Place and Bickenhall Street. We were responsible for Bickenhall Mansions, Montagu Mansions, Bryanston Mansions and Portman Mansions. This was, I realised, a major step up from the relative backwoods of Highgate to the West End of London, and I revelled in the challenge. And challenge it indeed turned out to be, because once Mr. Briggs realised that I was reasonably competent, we saw less and less of him. 'We' comprised our secretaries, Carol and

Tina, wages clerk David, four head porters (inevitably, resplendent in their uniforms), various under—porters and workmen. I spent the first few weeks getting to know everybody and building up a rapport with them, and enjoyed a good working relationship with everybody as a result.

In November, a crowd of us went to see Spike Milligan in 'Son of Oblomov', and marvelled at his mastery of the ad lib. (script?—what script?) and I continued enjoying Michelle. (Bi-lingual joke. A gendarme is patrolling the streets of Paris one night. He shines his torch down an alleyway and sees a bloke standing against a wall with his willy in his hand. 'Defense de pisser' says the gendarme. 'Je ne pisse pas, Je m'abuse' says the man. 'Pardon monsieur' says the gendarme 'Vive le sport').

Christmas Eve was spent at a party at Nick and Sue's flat, and Christmas Day was once again a family affair at Rockville.

Chapter Seven

Before we all knew it, it was 1966, which was to prove another exciting year. On 21st January, George Harrison married the model, Patti Boyd, at Epsom Registry Office. Little did I know that it would be the site of my second marriage, over fifteen years later. On my visits round the properties that Key Flats managed, the Head Porter at Portman Mansions told me about a small flat at the back of block 5, and I asked to see it. It was called 'The Studio', and was situated up a flight of iron stairs over a boiler house. It had a small entrance hall, a bed-sitting room, kitchen and bathroom, which had a close-up view of Baker Street Station, and I immediately fell in love with it. I told Mr. Briggs that, if I could live there, I would be much more efficient as an assistant manager; he made enquiries on my behalf, and arrangements were made for me to live there rent free for as long as I was employed at the Branch. On 31st January, a week after my twenty sixth birthday, I moved in. Bliss!

Around this time, I had been admiring adverts for a new style telephone, called a Trimphone. It came in a variety of pastel colours, was very slim, and its ringtone was not dissimilar to the sound of a budgie drowning. I applied for one, and a month later became one of the first people on the Welbeck exchange to own one.

(My own rent-free flat in the West End AND a Trimphone—could things possibly get any better?—very probably). In March, Cilla Black had a top ten hit with 'Alfie', and Mum and I went to see Michael Caine in the film. Interestingly, he had not been the first choice for the part, but two or three actors, one of whom was Laurence Harvey, had turned the part down because of the powerful and dramatic abortion scene. Abortion was currently illegal, and the law would not be changed until 1968. (more of Alfie later—six years later).

Although I was settling into the flat nicely, I was still travelling back to North London regularly. Whilst rehearsing in the West End for 'She Stoops to Conquer', Viv and I were also rehearsing in North London, so I was in and out of Baker Street Tube Station at all hours. One evening, after a frazzled journey back from Bounds Green, I popped in to the café for a coffee and espied a dark haired senorita behind the counter. She was in her late thirties, with an inviting smile, and I vowed to get to know her (but life was hectic, and she would have to wait her turn). By the end of April, however, her turn had come. We performed 'The Happiest Days of Your Life' on Friday and Saturday 22nd and 23rd, and I was back in the office on Saturday morning. I collected Mercedes (for that was her name, and it was to be my first experience of a used Mercedes) and took her over to North London for the after show party at Justin and Michelle's. I ran her home in the early hours, got to bed in the flat at seven a.m., to be up at one o'clock for Viv's arrival. We had a quick bite, then off to rehearsal in Victoria. Viv then beetled off back to North London, and I decided to wind down over a drink in the Globe, just opposite Baker Street Tube. Propping up the bar was Peter, the stoker. His job at Key Flats was to ensure that all the boilers to the various blocks were working efficiently. He was (like Chief Superintendent Bert Sparks) about six foot five with shoulders to match, but he had what Peter Cook would have described as a serious deficiency in the arm department—he only had one. (I never did discover why a one-armed man would choose a career as a stoker). He was a real gentle giant and I am pleased to say we got on very well. We had a drink together, and I repaired to bed.

On Friday 11th May, we did the first performance of 'She Stoops to Conquer' in a theatre in Whitehall Place, and the second performance on Saturday 12th, after which

Viv and I dashed back to North London for a party at Eve and Frank's house. I think Graham and Melanie must have had a tiff there, because I ran Melanie home in the early hours of Sunday morning, and then drove back to the flat. After about four hours kip I packed, and within half an hour Viv arrived and we set off for Victoria, where we met the whole company for 'She Stoops', and set off for Dover. From Dover we caught the ferry for Ostend, and spent most of Sunday travelling through Bruges, Brussels and Salzburg, arriving in Graz later that evening. On the Tuesday, we rehearsed at a school in the morning, and did our first performance on foreign soil that evening. We did two more performances in Graz, then left for a tour of Vienna on Thursday, arriving in Krems that evening. On Friday we did a matinee and an evening performance—the show was being received fairly well, but the four leads (the romantic interest) were not that strong, and we were not getting rave reviews. Saturday was a day off, which we spent touring, visiting Melch, and sailing up the Danube. On Sunday we travelled to Linz, and were greeted by a crowd of students amongst whom was the pulchritudinous Dagmar (sorry to be so sesquipedalian,) but I was suddenly smitten. I felt (very immodestly, I must admit) that I had also caught her eye, and so it was to prove. We did a matinee on Monday, and I spent a blissful evening dancing with Dagmar. We did another matinee on Tuesday, and I spent an even more blissful evening dancing decadently with the delightful Dagmar (sorry, a nasty attack of the alliteratives there). On Wednesday morning, we visited the school whose pupils had watched yesterday's matinee, and one of those magical moments that only happens once in a lifetime occurred. The whole cast were introduced one by one i.e. 'This is John Roth, who played Tony Lumpkin', and eventually they got to me. Now I was the only one who looked better offstage than on—all the other members of the cast appeared onstage dressed up to the nines in beautiful costumes, with extravagant wigs and colourful make-up. I, however, was playing a seventy year old servant in a dowdy costume, pale make-up and a bald wig. When they introduced me as follows 'and this is Tony Shelton, who played Diggory', there was an audible gasp of disbelief. (How could this upright, handsome young lad possibly be that wizened old man we saw yesterday, they thought). We (or at least, I), basked in their approbation for the rest of the afternoon and in the evening it was more terpsichore with Dagmar.

On Thursday, after exchanging addresses, I said a sad adieu to Dagmar and she promised to come to England in the near future. We left Linz and travelled to Erlangen for our final performance. When we eventually arrived at the theatre, I could hardly believe my eyes; it was the most beautiful theatre I had ever seen. It was called the Markgrafentheater, and was all red plush and gold leaf, and it was packed to the rafters with students studying the play for their A levels (or the German equivalent thereof); the atmosphere was absolutely electric. Act One went alright, but as the audience were all virtually word perfect, any slight lapse on an actor's part did not go unpunished; Act Two went in a similar fashion, but the audience were clearly not happy with John G., who was playing Hastings, and at the start of Act Three he got his come-uppance. He strode on, looking for his young lady, who had disappeared, along with a crowd of us, into the woods. His opening line was 'What a fool am I, to think that I could find them in this light', but he only got as far as 'What a fool am I' when he got stopped by laughter and sarcastic applause. Further on into the scene, another of those magical moments that only occurs once in a lifetime (or in this case, twice in a week) happened. I was meant to be halfway up a tree, but was in fact standing on a stool, holding a long pole with a lantern on the end of it, helping Mrs. Hardcastle find her daughter. I gingerly extended one wizened leg, thought better of it, and retracted it, my face creased with worry that I was stuck in this tree for good. This bit of business earned a standing ovation which stopped the show. I eventually came down from a head-swollen high (and the tree) and the show ended to polite, but not ecstatic, applause. We all went out for dinner later and, over the fast flowing wine, discussed the perils of performing to an audience who knew the play better than we did.

On Saturday, we spent the day in Erlangen in pouring rain. This, however, could not dampen our enthusiasm for the beerfest to which we had been invited, nor my enthusiasm for a tasty German wench called Christina. We all drank too much, I ogled Christina, we swapped addresses, and the company left later that night for Nuremberg. We travelled all of Sunday, and having said our farewells at Victoria, I eventually got back to the flat about nine o'clock that evening, exhausted and ecstatic in about equal measure.

Monday was a Bank Holiday, and I went back home to sunbathe before lunch with the family. I regaled them with stories of my trip, and spent the afternoon with Mum and Kay at a local fete, before returning to the flat at a respectable hour.

The following Monday, I had dinner with Eve and Frank. Later Frank and I went to weightlifting classes. Frank was attending weightlifting classes to become strong enough to beat me up if I got fresh with his wife (who—me?), and I was attending weightlifting classes to be strong enough to defend myself if Frank wanted to beat me up because he thought I was getting fresh with his wife (as if!). My volatile relationship with Frank never descended into outright violence, but one evening it came very close; Mark and I had been invited to a party in Finchley, and, when we arrived, Eve spotted me, shouted 'Tony!' and rushed over to me and kissed me passionately on the mouth. Mark looked on with an expression of wonderment and envy. We were later standing in the kitchen having a beer when Frank walked over to me and said 'What's going on with you and my wife?' I was just about to reply when he hit me round the face—not a punch, more a slap. I just stood there and raised a languid eyebrow, as if to say 'What are you playing at, you silly little man?' This infuriated him, and he screamed at me, then suddenly turned on his heel and strode off. (The raised languid eyebrow was later used by Roger Moore to great effect in the Bond Films; indeed, some people thought it was the highlight of his of his acting career).

The following evening, Mercedes threatened to call, but didn't. I fell asleep in the bath, and was awoken by the sound of a budgie drowning—no, I was mistaken. It was Eve telephoning for a chat.

Early in July, I popped in to see Nick and Sue in their flat over Bounds Green Tube Station, which they still shared with Desdemona, and later ran Mum and Dad to Luton Airport in Mum's Morris 1100 and collected Kay from her flat on the way back. On Sunday, I had lunch cooked for me by the wife of the head porter at Portman Mansions; she had registered that I was sometimes on my own on a Sunday, and had offered to provide lunch for me now and again. I was looking after Mum's 1100, and was also wrapped up in the drama scene. I was also seeing a lot of Viv—as with Jill, there was no sexual spark, but we enjoyed each other's company enormously. On Monday I took her to lunch at Le Petit Montmartre, and in the evening took Kay's friend Lesley to see 'The Wrong Box', with Peter Sellers and Michael Caine. On Tuesday I presented myself for babysitting duties in Southwood Lane, and on Wednesday I was with Eve and Frank at their place. Things were a bit volatile between Eve and Frank (surprise, surprise) and late on the evening of Sunday 19th July she phoned asking for help. I drove over to Barnet and took her to stay with friends for the night—Frank was nowhere to be seen. I took Eve to work in the morning and took her to dinner in the Deerstalker.

The swinging sixties were really swinging now, and the jewel in the crown was, for many people, the fact that England were hosting the football World Cup. Our first game, on 11th July, was against Uruguay, who held us to a goalless draw. Five days later, we beat Mexico 2-0, and then four days after that we beat France 2-0. On Saturday

I went back to Rockville, and after a gathering at Eve and Frank's place, I collected Kay and we drove up to Luton Airport to collect Mum and Dad; guess what –they had been diverted to Heathrow! They eventually got home on Sunday morning and I went back to the flat that evening. I lunched with Sue on Monday, Louise (from the Crown Drama Group) on Tuesday and rehearsed at St. Saviours on Thursday. After work on Saturday morning, I collected Mercedes and we drove over to North London, first to Janice's flat, then on to Eve and Frank's place. In the early hours of Sunday morning, Mercedes and I drove back to the Studio for nooky, and then I ran her home. I eventually got into bed at about 4 a.m. England had beaten Argentina 1-0 in a bad-tempered quarter final match, after which Alf Ramsey famously described the Argentinians as 'animals'.

On Tuesday I went round to Bruce's flat in Highgate where we had dinner before watching England beat Portugal 2-1 in the semi final. Rehearsals again on Thursday, then on Saturday I went round to Bruce's flat again to watch history being made—England beat West Germany 4-2 in the World Cup Final at Wembley, in front of almost 97,000 spectators. A thrilling match, an advert for all that was exciting about football. The Germans opened the scoring, and Geoff Hurst equalised just before half time. Martin Peters made it 2-1, and it looked as though England were home and dry. The Germans had other ideas, however, and equalised in the last minute of normal time. Geoff Hurst scored England's third, controversial, goal to make it 3-2. Seconds before the final whistle, some spectators got onto the pitch, causing Kenneth Wolstenholme to say 'Some people are on the pitch, they think it's all over', then, as Hurst thumps the ball into the back of the net, he emphatically completes his immortal phrase 'It is now!' Hurst became the first player to score a hat-trick in a World Cup final, which at the time was the most watched television programme ever. Interesting now to note that the England manager was English, the team was exclusively white, the players were not overpaid prima donnas, and the team, led brilliantly by the majestic Bobby Moore, played cohesively together, in front of arguably the best goalkeeper in the world, Gordon Banks. How times change.

On Sunday I collected Julie (remember her from El Toro?) and took her back to the Studio. We had not had a terrific time on our first date at Jill's party, and I wanted to make amends. I did so, and my abiding memory of the evening was her pale green diaphanous knickers, which were exactly the same colour as my bathwater after an infusion of Badedas.

On Wednesday, I popped in to see Mum and Dad, collected Janice from her flat from where we drove to Victoria to collect Dagmar, who arrived looking as lovely as ever. She was staying with Janice, and on Thursday I collected her in order to introduce her (show her off?) to everybody at St. Saviours. On Friday I had another Badedas moment with Julie, and on Saturday I took Dagmar to a party at Eve and Frank's house. Monday was a day off, so I collected Dagmar and took her for lunch in Potters Bar and a long walk in the country in the afternoon. On Thursday she came to the office and I took her home for dinner with Mum and Dad (hang on a minute—are we getting serious here?) then on to rehearsal. We were getting along swimmingly, but she did not approve of my smoking and wagged a disapproving Austrian finger at me every time I lit up. We were seeing each other almost every day, and on Saturday, 20th. August we teamed up with Bruce and Monica to attend Ken's wedding to his Greek girlfriend, Linda.

Unfortunately, things with Dagmar were now starting to deteriorate; not only did she not approve of my smoking, she also didn't approve of my bachelor lifestyle. At the time, I saw nothing wrong in smoking—my parents, most of my friends, the Beatles, film stars—they all seemed to smoke. We didn't know then the damage we were doing to ourselves. You were right, Dagmar, and it took me until 1984 to kick the habit. She was an old fashioned girl (which is why our courtship was chaste) who I think might have contemplated marrying me; unfortunately, she came along at a time when I was still enthusiastically sowing my wild oats. My diary entry for Thursday 25th August reads 'Straight home by tube for dinner. Out in Mum's Morris 1100 to see Dagmar, and to try and patch things up. All to no avail. Back to 165, then back to the flat by tube'. I think she had fallen in love with me in Austria, but had fallen out of love with me in England.

Bruce had now bought himself an Mk.9 Jaguar, and we spent August Bank Holiday Monday driving around North London feeling full of ourselves. On Thursday, I met Janice and Dagmar at Victoria to see Dagmar off; we said our goodbyes and I never saw her again.

Life goes on, however; from Victoria, I went straight to Paddington to catch the train to Bristol, where John met me. I spent a couple of days with him and Sandra, and returned to the Studio on Saturday afternoon. In the evening I went to a party at John Roth's place (he had played Tony Lumpkin in 'She Stoops') then on to Justin and Michelle's house for a late dinner.

Later that week I received a letter from German Christina, threatening to come over to England to see me, and had lunch with Joyce, the wife of the stage manager of the Crown Drama Group. On Wednesday 14th September, Bruce called at the flat in the evening, washed his hair, had a bath and then departed (cheeky sod). Later that month, I popped over to see him at his flat, and we drove over to see Eve in his Jaguar. We then moved on to Justin and Michelle's, where I stayed the night. (Don't ask about the sleeping arrangements—oh, come on, this is the swinging sixties).

I received another letter from Christina and continued rehearsing twice a week at St. Saviours. Late in October, I received a letter from Dagmar, but I now have no recollection of what it said. On Friday and Saturday we performed 'The Peaceful Inn', which apparently went down well—well, at least nobody asked for their money back.

There was a young actor from Bude

Who appeared on the stage in the nude

A voice from the stalls

Shouted out 'Balls'

Just like that—right out loud—wasn't that rude?

On 1st November, I received a third letter from Christina, and on 8th I received a fourth letter (what the hell did the girl find to write about—why didn't she rush round to the flat and show me her tattoos?). We had now started rehearsals for 'The House by the Lake', and on 3rd December (you're not going to believe this) I received a fifth letter from Christina. On Wednesday 7th Bruce phoned 'having written off the Jag'. He had not been hurt, but the car and his pride had taken a bashing.

One evening after a rehearsal, a crowd of us piled into the car I was driving at the time, and went to a pub in Crouch End for a couple of pints. At closing time we all emerged, got back into the car, and drove off towards Muswell Hill. As I drove past a stationary bus, a bloke ran out in front of it, and I hit him fair and square. He flew up into the air and was thrown over to the other side of the road. I was horrified at what had happened, and just sat there, stunned. He got up, rushed over to me, and said 'Are you alright, mate?' I had just knocked him for six, and he's asking me if I'm alright! 'Please don't feel guilty' he said, 'it was all my fault. I ran out in front of the bus without looking, but luckily I knew how to land'. I offered him a lift home, and we all had a cup of tea at his flat, before shaking hands and resuming our journey. Had the police been involved, it might have been a different story.

The actress Peggy Mount had now moved in to a flat in Montagu Mansions, and when she came down to my office one day, she told me she was rehearsing for her role in Cliff's next film 'Finders Keepers'—would I care for a couple of tickets to the premiere? Yes I would, Peggy, yes I would. Bruce and I hired dinner suits and went to the premiere on 8th December at the Odeon, Leicester Square. (Astonishingly, nobody mistook us for Cliff and Hank).

The long term resident of a flat in another block, Bryanston Mansions, was a Jewish lady called Bella Sherman, who suffered from elephantiasis. She was, as you might expect, absolutely enormous and rarely ventured out of her flat. She had been one of the very first people Mr. Briggs had introduced me to when I started at Baker Street and, whenever he was not in his office, (which was increasingly often) he could usually be found in her flat. She was a charming lady, and I got called out on more than one occasion to help her out with a problem. On Monday 19th December, I went out in the evening for a drink with Mr. Briggs, David and Carol from the office, and two of the Head Porters, and on Tuesday went back to Highgate to babysit for Alan and Judy. I spent the evening alone, but chatted up a girl on the tube on the way back to the flat.

On Christmas Eve I collected Kay's friend Lesley and took her to a party at Bruce's flat. I ran her home the next morning, then had a drink with Bruce and his parents. Back home to Rockville for Christmas lunch, and in the evening Dad's sister Jessie and her husband Sid, cousin Michael and his mother came round for the evening. Boxing Day was spent at home, and Kay's friends Barbara and Lesley called in the evening, and I later went out with John and Sandra and some friends of theirs.

And so another year was gone—and what a year it had been. I had moved in to a rent-free flat in the West End, sown the seed of one day acting in 'Alfie', toured Austria and Germany, stopped the show with a standing ovation, met Dagmar and Christina, watched England win the World Cup, went to a West End film premiere, and had more girls than I knew what to do with. (It could only be downhill from now on).

Chapter Eight

Nineteen sixty seven started with Dad coming up to the flat to help me decorate—the flat was now looking very smart—so smart, in fact, that Bruce and Monica spent the evening there while I was doing overtime in the office. (I have no idea what they got up to. I lie—I know exactly what they got up to, because Bruce insisted in telling me in graphic—should that be pornographic?—detail).

It was about this time that I met Tricia. She and Baxter and Mike had joined the drama group while we were rehearsing for 'The House by the Lake' and I was to get involved with all three of them (in vastly different ways). Tricia was a black haired beauty with a voluptuous figure and cut glass accent, and I immediately made a play for her. She was quite cool with me, saying she had no intention of getting involved with me while we were doing a play together (was that a sign I was in with a chance when the play had finished? Read on.) The first night I took her home to Barnet in Mum's car, I asked if I could kiss her goodnight. 'No' was the polite answer. I asked again the following night, and received the same answer. I asked again the third night, and received the same answer.

To celebrate my birthday, Lesley took me to lunch, and I went out for a drink in the Minstrel Boy in the evening with Tricia, Viv and Baxter. After sending all those letters, Christina finally did the decent thing and turned up in the flesh (and, oh boy—what flesh). I took her to the Post Office Tower, Burlington Gallery, then on to see 'What's New, Pussycat' with Peter Sellers, Peter O'Toole and Woody Allen (my favourite twenty seconds of the whole film went as follows):

Woody's friend.	'What are you up to then, Woody?'
Woody.	'I've got a job in a strip club, helping the girls in and out of their costumes'.
Woody's friend.	'What's the money like?'
Woody.	'Twenty five dollars a week'.
Woody's friend.	'That's not much'.
Woody.	'No—it's all I can afford'.

We rounded off the evening with a couple of pints in the Allsop Arms. Bruce decided he had so enjoyed entertaining Monica in my flat that he did it again the following week, and the next evening I entertained Christina. The following morning I took her to Victoria, and she caught the train back to Germany.

Her stay had been short, but very sweet.

Early in February, we had the dress rehearsal for 'The House by the Lake', and I later ran Tricia home in Mum's car. I escorted her to her door, and asked if I could kiss her goodnight, and guess what—she said YES!—so I gave her a quick peck on the cheek, jumped into the car, and roared off into the night. The balance of power had changed, and it was a good feeling. We performed 'The House by the Lake' on Friday and Saturday, and after the Saturday performance, Tricia, Baxter, Viv, Mike and his girlfriend Lilian, Mark and his wife Christine, Kay, Jean and I went back to the Studio for a party. Everybody but Tricia left at around midnight, when she promptly got undressed and jumped into bed. For the first time in my life I was shaking with nerves, and had to be cajoled into joining her. I ran her home in the early hours, and returned to the flat a very tired and very happy young man.

Things with Tricia went from good to wonderful and on Sunday 16th I was invited over to Barnet for a drink with her and her brother, followed by an enormous lunch cooked by her mother.

I had to work on the following Saturday morning, after which Tricia arrived. We had lunch, then repaired to the Studio for some afternoon delight. (I can't stand the record, but the delight was delightful).

John and Sandra had decided to tie the knot, and had asked me to be best man, so I decided to give them one of my abstract paintings as a wedding present. (I'm not sure what they thought of it, but it had pride of place on their lounge wall for many months).

There was a young fellow called Tony
Whose knees were exceedingly bony
He thought he could paint
But Dali he ain't
And he talked a load of baloney.

On Good Friday, John's Mum and Dad, his sister Kim, Tricia, Mark and I drove down to Bristol to celebrate. We did so in style, and spent the night at John's new house. The wedding went as planned, I delivered a reasonably funny speech (having overcome an attack of nerves) and Mark ran Tricia and me back to her house, then me back to Rockville. I continued seeing Tricia, and she would come up to the flat as often as I went over to Barnet. She often used to dress in a mini-kilt, black polo-neck sweater and black tights, and looked absolutely sensational. At the end of the month, Mrs. Sherman was discharged from hospital, and I had dinner and a couple of snorters with her in her flat. On April Fool's Day, Mike, Lillian, Tricia and I went out in

Mike's car, and Tricia and I later went back to the flat for another delightful interlude, after which I ran her home in the early hours of the morning. I went back to Barnet the following morning and took her home for lunch with Mum and Dad.

The following week I took Viv to see Antonioni's 'Blow Up', with David Hemmings in the lead. It was the first example of female full frontal nudity in mainstream cinema (with Vanessa Redgrave showing us everything else she had apart from acting ability).

Later that month we performed 'The Good Young Man', but a few of us were getting the feeling that it was time to start our own drama group. We didn't feel we had enough say in what plays were done and felt we ought to be a bit more 'cutting edge' and I was aware that the choice of plays was limited because it was a church society.

On 26th I met Tricia at Bounds Green tube and took her home for dinner with Mum and Dad (things are getting cosy again) then down to Wood Green to see another showing of 'A Young Man's Fancy'. The following evening we all attended the St. Saviours A G M and made our feelings known. It was the beginning of the end.

On 1st May Elvis married Priscilla Beaulieu in Las Vegas. Their courtship had lasted longer than their marriage would.

We had by now started our breakaway drama group and the first people to join us were a married couple called Phil and Connie. They were both teachers and a bit older than us, and it was Phil who suggested that we call ourselves 'The Thalians' after Thalia, the Greek muse of comedy.

At the end of May I had lunch with Melanie. Things were obviously not working out with Graham, and that evening she came up to the flat to be consoled. (I was getting very good at consoling unhappy wives.)

June and July were spent dashing from the Studio to Rockville and Barnet, and intensive rehearsals for the Thalians first production, a thriller called 'The Big Killing', which Baxter was directing, and which featured Phil, Mark, Mike, Viv, Tricia and me. We performed it at my old school in Rhodes Avenue on 21st and 22nd July and it was a resounding success.

At the end of the month I took Tricia to see Sean Connery in 'You Only Live Twice' (did you know that the screenplay was written by Roald Dahl?) Graham called early in August. Things were obviously not working out with Melanie, and that evening he came up to the flat to be consoled.

On the Friday of that week I spent a lovely evening at Tricia's house and stayed the night. The following morning we drove in to town and joined up with Mark and Christine and drove down to the Festival Theatre in Chichester to see 'An Italian Straw Hat'—a very funny farce. Then on to Bognor and home via Arundel and a couple of pubs. I again spent the night at Tricia's house. Looking back on our affair after all these years, I hadn't realised at the time how intense it was. We were spending virtually all our time together, and were besotted with one another; heady days and nights, indeed. However, what I now find utterly amazing is that I had booked a holiday for ten days in Spain, and it never once occurred to me to invite her to join me. Mum, Dad and Tricia ran me to the airport on Sunday, and I spent a sun-drenched ten days in Calella. The first voice I heard on my return was Tricia's, when she rang to wake me up on Thursday morning. It was all about to go pear-shaped, however. We were now regarded by everybody as a couple, and somebody made a remark one evening about us probably becoming a married couple. I made a flippant retort, somewhere along the lines of 'You must be joking'. I now realise that this must have hurt Tricia enormously, because I think marriage might well have been on her mind, though it had never once occurred to me—I was having far too much fun (most of it with her, admittedly), and generally being too selfish.

And so Saturday 16th September turned out to be a momentous, and very unhappy day. Mum and Dad drove off to Scotland for a holiday, it was Eve's birthday, and Tricia gave me the boot. She, Eve and Tony came up to the flat, where she announced it was all over between us. She left on her own, and Eve and Tony stayed to console me—I needed consoling, because for the first time in my life I cried over a girl. (the consoler consoled—I suppose it was inevitable).

To put my problems into perspective, however, Mum, now fifty nine, had been diagnosed with breast cancer and had a mastectomy. She recovered physically, but started to suffer bouts of depression, which led, in due course, to a mental breakdown. She started day care at Halliwick Hospital, where she met the afore-mentioned Mr. Digby, and a girl called Ruth. Looking back now, I realise how selfish and self-centred I had been. I was upset over the break-up with Tricia (which had been caused by my boorish behaviour and thoughtlessness), but uninvolved to any worthwhile extent with Mum's physical and mental state. Dad and Kay had been much more caring, as indeed they were in the years to come when Mum's cancer returned, and they nursed her at home in her final weeks.

The month continued with rehearsals, meetings with Viv (we were still trying to get this bloody farce written) and Melanie who came up to the flat one evening to console me, rather than the other way round. Somebody new on the scene was a young lady called Gill from South Africa, who was staying with Freda and Stuart. Upon meeting her, I immediately invited her to a party, and on Saturday 30th September Justin, Michelle, Gill, sundry others and I went to the party at Carol's house, where I stayed the night with Gill. She was a delightful girl and I have particularly fond memories of her firm pert buttocks (if you are down in the dumps after having been ditched, I can really recommend getting to grips with a pair of firm pert South African buttocks). In fact, I was so smitten with her buttocks that I took them to see Warren Beatty and Faye Dunaway in 'Bonnie and Clyde'.

October continued the theme of previous months; writing with Viv, rehearsing with the usual suspects and horizontal work-outs with Gill and Melanie, et al. Not only was I writing with Viv, we were lunching and dining on a regular basis, and after lunch on Monday 16th., we went to the patents office at Chancery House.

As well as the painting, I loved sketching (particularly caricatures), and had recently created two cartoon characters called Bert and Fred; Bert was a long streak of cat's piss, dressed from head to foot in black with a top hat, and Fred was a fat git, dressed from head to foot in black with a bowler hat. I decided to have some plaster models made, to be used as wall plaques, and displayed them in the Studio as an antidote to the trio of flying ducks, which were very popular at the time (and, in my opinion) exceedingly naff. I never did get around to arranging a patent, and poor Bert and Fred never found fame as the 'in' wall decoration.

With Bruce at Terry and Sue's wedding.

My programme design for 'Don't Utter a Note'.

At Rockville with Mark, Christine, Viv and Mary after the
Saturday performance of 'The Happiest Days of Your Life'.

Rehearsing the woodland scene, which would
earn me a standing ovation...

…at the lovely Markgrafentheater.

With Bruce, Monica and Dagmar at Ken and Linda's wedding.

German Christina in the flesh.

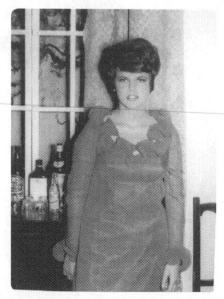

Tricia, at her beautiful best, on the set of 'The Big Killing'.

Bert and Fred
Still going strong after
all these years!

Bert and Fred.

Eve and Tony were still on the scene, but Frank seemed to have disappeared. So her husband was out of the way but my namesake was now escorting her. Bugger! After all the rehearsals, we finally performed 'For Better, For Worse', and yet another production was put to bed.

Kay had had a succession of jobs, all of which had been office-bound, and which she had found unfulfilling; she decided to be adventurous, and applied to join the police. She was accepted, and joined the Met in November. The women's trainee Section House was Peto House, not far from me in Chiltern Street, and I regularly got involved with running her between there and Peel House.

Mike was now working for Islington Borough Council, and soon discovered that the lovely old theatre in Hoxton was available for hire. We started to use it for rehearsals, and would eventually do a play and an old time music hall there.

After a particularly good party at Mike L's flat on the Saturday, it was up relatively early to go Terry and Sue's baby daughter's christening—a lovely girl called Claire. And once again it was suddenly Christmas. I spent a lazy Christmas Eve with Mike, Lilian and Viv playing cards, and went to see Justin, Michelle, Eve and Frank (Frank? Was he back on the scene?) on Christmas morning, then back to Rockville for the rest of the day with the family. Not a particularly happy time, but at least we were together as a family.

Chapter Nine

Nineteen sixty eight got off to an inauspicious start. For our second Thalian production, we decided to perform 'Variation on a Theme' by Terence Rattigan, and Tricia and I were both cast. I felt extremely embarrassed that everybody must have known that she had given me the boot, and the situation was made worse by the fact that Des O'Connor had a big hit with a sad song called 'Everybody Knows'. The play, directed by Baxter, was performed early in January to lukewarm reviews and was not one of our better or happier productions. Tricia left the group, and the rest of us immediately started rehearsals for 'Trap for a Lonely Man' in Hoxton.

After her training at Peto House, Kay started her career proper on 12th. February in Harlesden. The following week, Bruce and I spent the evening in a beer keller, where we managed to pull three girls (one and a half each?—how does that work?—answers on a postcard, please). On 21st. February, after dining with Mark and Christine at their house, I joined a crowd to celebrate Mike's stag night. We performed 'Trap for a Lonely Man' on Friday, and Mike and Lilian got married on Saturday morning. We all had tea at Baxter's flat in the afternoon, and did the second performance of the show that evening.

The following week, Bruce, Mark and I took the three girls from the beer keller for a drink in the Allsop Arms and then back to the flat. (What—only one each this time?). We were now rehearsing for 'See How They Run', a wartime farce by Philip King, and were increasingly using the facilities in Hoxton. On one occasion, after a rehearsal in the theatre, we all repaired to the local pub for a drink. It was quite a seedy place, inhabited by some very dodgy looking characters, and the entertainment (such as it was) was provided by the customers, who were invited up to the mike to sing a song of their choice. One of the regulars, an unsavoury looking character strolled over to our table and said to me 'And what are you going to sing for us?' 'I don't, er, I don't sing' I stammered. 'You do if you come into this pub' he said. 'I'd really rather not' I replied. He came up close to me, got hold of my lapels, and, with his other hand, withdrew a knife from his jacket pocket, which he placed gently against my throat. 'I know', I said, 'I'll sing 'Yellow Submarine'. I got up, went to the microphone, gave an appalling rendition, and returned to the table, visibly shaking. The man with the knife gave me a curt nod, as if to indicate that I had passed some sort of initiation test. We did not use the pub again.

Baxter had been living in a flat in Grosvenor Road, Muswell Hill, but decided to move in with his friend Colin. He, Baxter, had been having doubts about his sexuality, and was still not aware of which side of the fence he would end up on. Mike and Lilian rented Baxter's old flat and I enjoyed tea with them the day after they moved in. Later in the month I escorted Eve to John and Michelle's party where we stayed the night, and later still, Eve came up to the flat and we went to the Ideal Home Exhibition, followed by dinner at her place. I returned to the flat and turned in early. I was awoken from my slumbers by a warm female body wriggling next to me. Bruce, his on/ off employer and minicab firm owner Ralph, and Mark had been out on the town, and had pulled four girls (apparently thinking that if they were going to descend on the flat, they ought to bring one back for me).

In March, Cliff sang 'Congratulations', our entry in that year's Eurovision Song Contest, and, although he didn't win (he came second), he had his ninth number one single. (Thought—if he had come first, would that have constituted a case of Premature Congratulations?).

Early in April I had lunch with Viv in the Devonshire Arms, and the following day Mark and I took Carol and Tina from the office to lunch in the Barley Mow, and saw Paul and Ringo playing darts. The Beatles' office/shop in Baker Street, called Apple, was just a stone's throw from the pub and they used to pop in now and again for a pint.

On Monday 8th, Justin, Michelle and Viv came up to the flat for dinner, then we all trooped off to a hotel in Berners Street for the 'I Like Swipe' Campaign. This was the first example in this country of 'Pyramid Selling'. We all invested a small sum, but did not enjoy the promised wonderful returns, and only just got our money back.

Early in May, Bruce and I went to a rather unusual show at the Palladium; the first half was the Shadows, (great glasses, Hank) and the second half, not, as you might expect, Cliff, but Tom Jones. We witnessed the knicker throwing phenomenon at first hand.

Early the next morning, I met up with Mark to go to Clacton for the Key Flats day out. We missed the train we were supposed to catch, but eventually caught up with the Key Flats porterage and works staff and had a good boozy day at the seaside. The following day, I had dinner with Mark and Christine, followed by a few games of Scrabble; Wednesday found me escorting Gill to see 'Fantasia' at Studio One, and on Saturday Mum and I went to see 'Un home et une Femme' in Wood Green.

We had by now started rehearsals for 'Guilty Party', a boardroom drama, which were interspersed with bouts of Scrabble and an invitation to the one and only orgy I have ever attended. (Scrabble and an orgy—if it wasn't one organ getting exercise it was another —or so I fondly imagined). Justin and Michelle invited me and any broad-minded young lady along, and when Irish Gill and I got there we joined the host and hostess, and Ken and his wife Rose. Now my idea of an orgy is when a crowd of people all strip off and have group sex, but Justin had different ideas. He immediately swagged Rose upstairs, leaving Michelle, Ken, Gill and me in the lounge. As it wasn't the done thing to stick with the person you arrived with, Michelle and I cuddled up on the floor together; however, although I was seeing Justin and Michelle regularly, Michelle and I were now merely friends, the spark long having departed. Truth to tell, I was furious that Justin had whisked Rose (who I fancied like mad) off to another room. My sole orgy, therefore, was spent watching Ken enthusiastically service Gill. On the way home, I took it out on Gill, who was very apologetic, saying she thought that was what I had wanted. The fact is, I was in a sulk because things had not turned out the way I had hoped. (Some orgy!)

The next day I saw Eve in the afternoon, and took Gill to see Mark and Christine in the evening, and spent the night with her at the flat. At the end of the month I took Viv to see 'Elvira Madigan', the Swedish tragedy, in which slow motion and the slow movement from Mozart's piano concerto no. 21 were used to such magical effect.

We presented 'Guilty Party' on 2nd and 3rd of August, and our reputation was such that new members were flooding in. Thanks to Mike, who had seen what another amateur theatre group had done, we had become an evening class under the adult education scheme, and people were paying to join us. Three new recruits were Francesca, Eva and her young daughter Jenny. Jenny was a shy, naive fifteen year old schoolgirl, who fairly rapidly metamorphosed into the archetypal dolly bird—blonde hair, big boobs, miniskirt and boots, and I'm not really sure why she joined us. She never appeared on stage, but made a decorative addition to our group. Francesca and Eva both turned out to be competent actresses.

Back at Key Flats, Carol in the office decided to leave in September, and I spent a week interviewing for a new secretary. The girl who eventually got the job was called Lavinia; she was one of those girls who, without make-up, was quite plain, but with the rouge and mascara looked stunning. She proved to be a very efficient secretary, and before too long became a regular after hours visitor to the flat.

Things continued at the office at a leisurely pace; there were porters and workmen to supervise, potential employees and leaseholders to interview, all fairly predictable, run of the mill stuff until one Friday afternoon early in October, Tina came into my office and announced that a lady called Veronica would like to see me. I asked her to show her in, and in swept the tenant of an upper floor flat in Bickenhall Mansions. She explained that her husband spent a lot of time abroad, and that she was considering moving out or sub-letting the flat—could she discuss the matter with me? I said certainly, and we discussed the pros and cons of various options. I told her that if she were to vacate the flat, we would need to do a schedule of dilapidations, i.e checking the general condition of the flat. She asked if it would be convenient for me to pop up with her and have a look round, and I agreed. We went up to the flat, which turned out to be beautifully furnished and in very good decorative condition, and I told her that we would have no trouble finding a new tenant, if that were what she wanted. We got chatting, and I discovered that she was a hostess at the Victoria Sporting Club. She was in her thirties, Jewish, full of what the Jews call chutzpah (shameless audacity to you) and a stocky but very curvaceous figure. She asked if I would like a drink, and I said a cup of tea would go down a treat. 'I had something a little stronger in mind' she said, and disappeared fleetingly, only to reappear with a pair of large brandies. She then asked if would care to smoke, and I pulled out a pack of Benson & Hedges. 'I had something a little stronger in mind', she said, and offered me a joint. I had previously dabbled with cannabis on four or five occasions with varying results—it sometimes caused a pleasing feeling of euphoria, and sometimes had no effect at all. This time, however, coupled with the brandy, it had a wonderful effect, and I sat in her lounge with a contented smile on my face. While I telephoned Tina to tell her where I was if needed, Veronica poured more drinks and suggested we repair to the bedroom. We lay on her bed, she making sure I got a good view of her pink underwear, and we smoked and drank. After a while, she got up to replenish our drinks, and when she resumed her place on the bed I noticed that her pink underwear had vanished. I wasn't immediately sure if this was an optical illusion brought on by the combination of the brandy and cannabis, or if she were preparing to launch an all-out attack on me; the latter proved to be the case, and I was suddenly engulfed by arms, legs, boobs and other parts of her anatomy she thought might interest me. We spent an exhausting night, fuelled by copious amounts of brandy, interrupted by short breaks now and then for more joints. We lay in late the following morning, a Saturday, and I suddenly remembered I had a rehearsal that evening. Veronica announced that she would drive me there, and would be delighted to meet everybody. I had recently approached the actress, Diana Churchill, to be our President, and she had agreed. After seeing Veronica's imperious entrance, Christine enquired if this was our new President. 'Good God, no', I replied, and languished in a corner while Veronica went around introducing herself to everybody. We duly rehearsed, and she ran me back to the West End. By now I was exhausted and concerned for both my safety and sanity—any more nights like last night and I would be a gibbering wreck. While Veronica was parking the car, I ran back to the Studio and locked the door. Unfortunately, I had disclosed to her yesterday where I lived, and, within minutes, I heard footsteps on the staircase and a thunderous knocking on the door. I cowered in the bathroom and after a while she gave up and went away. After a couple of attempts to get to me on the Sunday, she got the message and backed off. I could not have lasted long at her pace.

Early in November, Mike L. and I put an ad in the Hornsey Journal for people interested in joining the Thalians, not specifically for budding actors and actresses, but people who might have some talent with regard to P.R. and building a good image for the group, and we got a response that was to prove life changing for a number of people. One interesting applicant was a chap called Brian, whom Mike and I interviewed, and welcomed into the group with open arms. After a couple of weeks, he brought his wife Yvonne and her friend Ruth along. Ruth was a beautiful dark haired art teacher with some fiery Welsh blood in her, but both Ruth and Yvonne had a history of mental problems and were attending Halliwick Hospital, where, incidentally, Ruth had already met Mum and Mr. Digby (remember him from the Thirlestane Garage? He had probably buckled under the strain of working for Mr. Gelber.) Anyway, Brian got involved with Viv, and Yvonne, unable to cope with the situation, committed suicide.

We were now involved in our first attempt at putting together an evening of one act plays under the umbrella heading of 'Murder'; the first play, a drama entitled 'Enter a Queen' by Michael Dines, directed by Justin, the second, a Victorian melodrama called 'Dark Brown' by Philip Johnson, directed by yours truly (my first attempt at directing), with music composed and played on the piano by Justin, and the third a drama entitled 'The Rats' by Agatha Christie, directed by Baxter. On the nights of the performances, 'Enter a Queen' was saved from oblivion by Francesca, who showed she had the stuff of which Shakespearean heroines are made; 'Dark

Brown' got the laughs it richly deserved, and as a result of my performance as the ludicrous Fred Whitworth I was nominated for (but didn't win) the Wood Green Weekly Herald Actor of the Year Award, and 'The Rats', a three-hander with Mike, Ruth and me was adjudged to be suitably thrilling.

We entered 'The Rats' into the London Borough of Enfield Annual Drama Festival and Ruth won the Best Actress Award. We later entered it into the Woking Drama Festival and collected yet more awards. The Saturday evening performance was graced by our President, Diana Churchill, and the after show party was a self-congratulatory affair, culminating in smoking, drinking, dancing, flirting and a silly game involving a spinning bottle.

Mum had been finding the journey to work in Palmers Green quite tiring, and had recently landed a job with Bent's Transport in Lordship Lane, Wood Green. This was to turn out quite a useful move, both for her and us. Baxter's Mum lived in Littlehampton, and invited him and some of his friends down for lunch. We managed to arrange the loan of a Bedford Dormobile from Bent's and one Sunday morning Bruce, Viv, Mike, Lilian, Louise, Baxter and I set off, with me at the wheel, for the coast. We had an excellent lunch, and in the afternoon discovered the Beach Hotel and the Windmill Theatre. Mike's mind went into overdrive, and the idea was born to put on shows at the theatre, and charge an all-inclusive price for the tickets and the transport from North London. More of this later.

Towards the end of November Baxter decided to hold a party. Mike and Lilian had now bought a house in Kingsley Road, Palmers Green, and Baxter was renting the flat in Muswell Hill Road. Bruce and I, for reasons best known to ourselves, decided to go in drag. We dressed ourselves up in high heels, tights, slinky long black dresses, wigs, and applied rouge and mascara with abandon. We drove the short distance from Rockville and made our entrance, and what an entrance! The usual crowd had grown used to all sorts of outrageous behaviour, both on and off stage, but the new recruits weren't quite so sure what to make of us. Were we transvestites, were we queer (gay still meant happy in those days)—whatever, Bruce ruined the illusion by flopping on to a sofa with his feet and knees eighteen inches apart. The party turned out to be one of the best, largely because the girls, for some strange reason, seemed to find us infinitely more sexy in drag than in our usual gear. I flirted with Christine, Jenny, Ruth and Rose (from the orgy), and arranged to see Rose at some future date.

On 25th November Bruce and I (dressed in male attire) went to see Cliff and the Shadows at the Palladium, and gave two young ladies a lift home. Wednesday evening was spent casting for our next production, 'Tobias and the Angel'. I spent some more time with Ruth working on the play and on Friday 13th December I gave her a lift home to Dartmouth Park Hill, then went back to spend the night at the Studio. The following evening was a most enjoyable dinner party at Mark and Christine's house. I stayed the night at Rockville (very handy, having all these beds to choose from) and returned to the Studio on Sunday evening.

When flats changed hands at our branch, we could usually find a new tenant from our long waiting list, but occasionally we used the services of an estate agent. Our preferred choice was a lady called Constance Barnett, a short, plump, bespectacled lady in her fifties and a formidable character to boot. I was invited to a cocktail party at her offices on the Monday, and attended a second cocktail party on the Tuesday at the Alfred Marks Bureau. I was not invited to either party because of my good looks, charisma and scintillating wit—it was because they thought (quite correctly) that I could put a lot of business their way.

I had lunch with Mary in the flat on the Wednesday, and that evening I had a drink with John's father, Ken. He had been the stage manager at St. Saviours for many years, and we chatted about this and that, and he expressed interest in how I was doing with our new group. Afterwards, I spent the night at Mark and Christine's house. On Tuesday, Christmas Eve, I had a lunchtime drink with everybody from the office, and took Eve out for a drink in the evening. I spent the night and the following day at Rockville, a very pleasant one with Mum, Dad, Kay, and her friend Jill, (no, I had nothing to do with this one).

Chapter Ten

On Thursday 30th January, 1969 the Beatles performed their legendary rooftop concert in London—it was to be their last live performance together, and it stopped the traffic, as they in turn were stopped by the police. I was in the office at the time, and with the window open, could actually hear them four or five blocks away.

Mike decided that we needed new members, especially a stage manager, and placed another of his ads in the local press. One of the people who replied was Jim, who joined us as actor and stage manager, and who was to become a stalwart for both the Thalians and North London productions.

On 2nd. March, Concorde made its first flight. It was the most beautiful aeroplane imaginable, and the first passenger aircraft to fly at twice the speed of sound. It was to be grounded, many years later, having delighted, amazed and infuriated people all over the world.

Lavinia decided to move on to pastures new, and Beryl Reid became the latest celebrity to move into Montagu Mansions. I had long been a fan of hers, and found her as charming and funny in real life as she was on the stage and in films. Diana Churchill announced that, because of work commitments, she could no longer continue to be our president; however, I had recently met the actor Bill Owen (best known for his television work in 'Last of the Summer Wine') and he agreed to become our next president. I was now courting Ruth, and, having realised what a good actress she was, soon discovered, to my chagrin, that she could drink me under the table.

On 12th March, much to the disgust of his female fans, Paul McCartney married Linda Eastman at Marylebone Town Hall.

Later that month, Bruce started work for Wolf Mankowitz as assistant, general dogsbody and driver; the driving involved chauffeuring Wolf around in his white E type Jaguar. A tough job, Bruce assured me, but somebody had to do it. Wolf's insurance document was the strangest I had ever seen, and went as follows: 'Classes of Person Entitled to Drive—anybody with Wolf Mankowitz's permission, but specifically excluding Wolf Mankowitz'. I presume he had never bothered to take a driving test.

Ruth and I were spending more and more time with each other, the only cloud on the horizon being her bouts of depression. I vowed that I would be able, over time, to cure her and make her happy. We were both busy rehearsing for 'Tobias and the Angel' (with me playing her father!), and I was increasingly thinking of asking her to marry me. One evening, while a crowd of us were discussing that evening's rehearsal, I asked Mike if I could borrow his car, and took Ruth for a drive. After an hour or so, I proposed, to Ruth's evident astonishment, but we continued driving and talking, and by the morning, she had come round to my way of thinking, and accepted. I ran Ruth home, returned the car to Mike and told him the news.

We performed 'Tobias and the Angel', with our new recruit Jim as stage manager, but it was only moderately successful.

With Bruce as best man, Ruth and I were married at Marylebone Town Hall on 25th April and went back to Ruth's parents' house for the reception. Just before we were due to leave for the Studio, the enormity of what she had done caused Ruth to lock herself in the bathroom, and it took the combined efforts of quite a few of us to entice her out. We eventually drove back to the Studio for our first night as a married couple. Mum had agreed to lend us her car for a week, and the following morning we drove off to Devon and Cornwall for our honeymoon.

Constance Barnett had recently found buyers for a couple of our flats, and asked me if I would like to work for her. I had been doing the job at Baker Street branch on auto-pilot for a while now, and realised that this might be the right time to take on a (potentially very lucrative) challenge. As a result, I left Key Flats on 4th July, and started work with Constance Barnett on 7th.

Bill Owen, our new president, was appearing in the West End in 'In Celebration', co-starring with Alan Bates, and offered us tickets and the chance to go backstage after the show. Ruth, being a real fan of Alan Bates, accepted with alacrity, and we went to see the show in July. Afterwards, Bill Owen took us backstage to Alan Bates' dressing room, and he appeared wearing a dazzlingly white towelling dressing gown. Unfortunately, he hardly noticed Ruth, and only had eyes for me. (Well I never!) This, however, did not deter Ruth from wanting to go and see him in the film 'Women in Love'. Mike and Lilian joined us, and we all thoroughly enjoyed the film, the undoubted highlight of which was the nude wrestling scene between Alan Bates and Oliver Reed.

Back in the world of the amateur theatre, the Thalians had decided to present 'The Bear', by Chekhov, as a starter, followed by 'Black Comedy', by Peter Shaffer as the main course. 'The Bear', one of Chekhov's rare comedies, was to be directed by Justin, and I was directing and acting in 'Black Comedy'. Jim invited his brother David to join us, and they both appeared in 'Black Comedy' to great comic effect, as did Eva, hilariously playing a gin-sodden wreck. This farce, to my mind, is one of the funniest ever written, easily on a par with Michael Frayn's 'Noises Off'. The theatrical device in this play is that the lighting is reversed. The bulk of the story is told while the lights are fused and the actors are supposed to be in total darkness, but during this time the stage lights are on, and when the lights are supposed to be on, the stage is in darkness. I am delighted to say we did the script proud 'The Bear' was roundly panned, but reviews for 'Black Comedy' were little short of ecstatic.

Shirley was a girl who had been a dancer in Paris, before moving to London to work behind the bar at the Intimate Theatre; tall and thin, with legs up to her armpits and a liking for acting and alcohol, she also fancied anything in trousers. She was round at Mike and Lilian's house one evening when I happened to call in for a drink or two. Recalling 'Women in Love', I challenged Mike to a bout of nude wrestling. Having had a couple of glasses of Scotch, he readily agreed, and we both stripped off and got down to it. Shirley could not believe her eyes, or her luck. I don't think she actually wet herself, but it was a close call.

Miriam and Reg had moved to a rented house in Henley, and invited Ruth and me for dinner. We caught the train and spent a very pleasant evening, and by the time we left, we were both feeling quite mellow. On the walk back to the station, however, we managed to fall out, and spent the journey back to North London in separate carriages; we were both strong willed, and neither of us would back down—stupid, or what?

Mark, although married, was always out for a bit on the side, and was currently seeing a girl called Sue. Sue was very friendly with a young couple called Tommy and Kate—Tommy was a serious individual, bespectacled, with thinning hair, and an abiding passion for the music of Gustav Mahler, and Kate was a very attractive dark haired teacher, much more vivacious than her husband. One evening, Mike and Lilian invited a large crowd, including Tommy and Kate and Ruth and me, to a party in Kingsley Road. Ruth and I hardly said a word to each other all evening, and at about ten o'clock, I found myself dancing with Kate in the garden. I kissed her, we exchanged numbers, and soon embarked on an affair that would last for years.

Wolf Mankowitz signed up to shoot a film in Israel, and asked Bruce to go with him. Bruce readily agreed, and asked him if I could look after his E Type while they were away, and, to our astonishment, he said yes. They jetted off to the sun, and I spent a fabulous week posing in the sexiest car in the world.

Work with Constance Barnett turned out to be very boring, and not very lucrative, and I faced the prospect of being imminently evicted from the Studio. By now, Ruth was pregnant and we were not exactly awash with money; we lived some of the time upstairs in Rockville and some of the time at her parents' house. Being in this impecunious state, the prospect of Cliff giving a free concert was quite appealing; he was heavily into his religion by now, and a pregnant Ruth and I went along to hear him sing some inspirational songs at his local church, St. Pauls in Finchley.

The Studio had now been let, and Christmas this year was split between Rockville with Mum and Dad, and Ruth's parents' house with her Mum and Dad.

Chapter Eleven

Laurence Harvey was born Larushka Mischa Skikne, a Lithuanian Jew, and he came to England to find fame and fortune as an actor. He changed his name to Laurence Harvey (after Harvey Nicholls, the department store), and soon became involved with the actress, Hermione Baddeley. He later married another actress, Margaret Leighton, but did not stay with her for long. He was trying to make his way in Hollywood, and after his performance in the film 'Room at the Top' he became a hot property. Whilst in Hollywood, he met and wooed Joan Cohn, the widow of the legendary film producer, Harry Cohn; as a result of his wealth, she had become arguably the richest woman in Hollywood. Harvey then found international fame as the killer in 'The Manchurian Candidate', alongside Frank Sinatra, and, after marrying Joan Cohn, enjoyed an enviable lifestyle. He came back to England in 1969, and signed to appear in 'Arms and the Man' and 'The Alchemist' by George Bernard Shaw. (Shaw was walking in London one day when a man approached him and asked 'Excuse me, are you Shaw?' 'Absolutely certain' came the reply.)

Bruce had now been working for Wolf Mankowitz for a while, and was thoroughly enjoying driving the E type and being on the periphery of show business circles. Mankowitz, a charming man and a good employer, was a big, unkempt Jew, who made his living as a scriptwriter and film producer (he had written the script for the first 'Casino Royale', the spoof Bond movie). He was a friend of Laurence Harvey, and when Harvey broke his knee during rehearsals for 'The Alchemist', Mankowitz asked Bruce if he knew anybody who would be interested in being his driver and dresser. Driving and the theatre, thought Bruce—I know just the chap. And so it was arranged that I would go to Harvey's suite at the Dorchester to be interviewed. He offered me the job on the spot and asked me to start work immediately. He told me he was about to go down to Chichester to appear as the lead in 'Arms and the Man', and that I would be expected to be with him for the length of the run. Regardless of the fact that I now had responsibilities in the shape of a pregnant wife, I accepted without hesitation. I told Constance Barnett what she could do with her job, and my first duty with Laurence Harvey was to drive him to a coachbuilders in West London to inspect the customised Mini he had ordered, but would not yet be able to drive. The following day, he asked me to deliver a package to an address in Hampstead. I did so, and the door was answered by Ringo, who said 'Ta very much'.

Christmas was spent with Ruth, splitting our time between my parents and hers, and on 2nd February 1970 our daughter Rebecca was born. I spent the time of the birth, not at Ruth's side, but with her mother in the hospital reception area, and we wet the baby's head in no uncertain fashion. We were now living in Dartmouth Park Hill with Ruth's parents, but in no time at all I was summoned by Laurence Harvey to pack and take him to Chichester. Ruth was understandably less than pleased at this development, and our marriage, less than one year old, was continuing on its rocky path.

I drove him down in his Sunbeam Rapier, and we booked in at the Chichester Motel (now the Ramada Chichester). Life was to become a routine of driving him in to the Festival Theatre to rehearse, getting to know the backstage staff, helping him in and out of costume, and driving him back to the hotel, before dining (usually alone), then bed. The members of the cast were, in their day, well known and well thought of; John Standing, who was to marry Brian Forbes and Nanette Newman's daughter, Sarah; Margaret Courtenay, a seasoned Shakespearean actress, Charles Lloyd Pack (the father of Roger Lloyd Pack, who was to find fame as 'Trigger' in 'Only Fools and Horses), and Sarah Badel, the daughter of Alan Badel, the matinee idol. They seemed to be a very happy company, and, during the run of the play, we were all invited to a party held by one of the backstage staff. It was after a matinee performance, and I drove Harvey the short distance to the house, where most of the others had already gathered. As we walked in, I was immediately struck by the distinctive aroma of cannabis and the sight of an already inebriated Margaret Courtenay encouraging young stage-hands to dance with her, (and we all know what horizontal activity dancing is a vertical expression of). I do apologise, I ended that sentence with a preposition (which differed from Margaret's sentences, all of which ended with a proposition). I fairly quickly spotted Molly, whom I had previously noticed backstage at rehearsals, and invited her into the garden for a chat. With a glass of wine in one hand, and a joint in the other, I regaled her with stories of my magical and unfailing prowess with impressionable young girls, only to be tapped on the shoulder and a voice asking 'Excuse me, are you Tony?'. This is it, I thought, her boyfriend has arrived and I am about to get thumped. 'Yes' I replied meekly. 'Mr. Harvey would like you to take him home now'. Relief washed over me, and I took my leave of Molly, hoping to renew our acquaintance at a later date.

I helped Harvey into the car, jumped into the driver's seat, and we set off. The effects of the wine and the cannabis now took over, and the road started coming at me in great waves; I realised immediately that the safest thing to do was to get back to our hotel in as short a time as possible, so I put my foot to the floor, which is where it stayed for the duration of the journey. We spent the next ten minutes riding the tarmac breakers and arrived back at the hotel, where the car settled down and I switched the engine off. As I helped Harvey out of his seat, he looked at me and said 'You drove well tonight'—it was the only comment he ever made about my driving.

Although married to Joan Cohn, Harvey was conducting an affair with Paulene Stone (who was also staying at our hotel), a model whose image was all over London at the time; she was the face of the White Horse whisky campaign ('You can take a White Horse anywhere'), and she was as beautiful as she was ubiquitous. One afternoon, Harvey summoned me up to his room. 'My wife has been on the telephone', he said, 'and she's on her way over from the States, so I want you to drive Paulene back to London this evening'.

I telephoned Ruth to say I would be home that evening. 'Why?' she asked. 'I'm driving the most beautiful woman in London back to her house in Hampstead' I said. There was an icy silence on the other end of the line, and I realised that it was not the most thoughtful thing I could have said to my new wife. I drove Paulene back to Hampstead, received a cool reception from Ruth, and drove straight back down to Chichester the following morning.

The job soon settled into a boring routine, and Harvey was not in the best of moods. He was parted from his mistress and his knee was causing him pain; eventually, we had a falling out over some trivial matter, and it was agreed we would part company. The following morning I packed my bags and his secretary, Sandy, drove me to the station, where I caught a train back to London. I was once again out of work, but this time with a wife and baby to support.

Our next production was 'Antigone', by Jean Anouilh, a Greek tragedy, directed by Baxter with Ruth playing the eponymous heroine and me playing her lover Haemon. We performed it in Hoxton, and Ruth was superb, but I was no more than adequate, and realised that I was much happier doing comedy.

My next job was to be a little less glamorous, delivering frozen chips to Wimpy Bars and the like in and around the West End. At about eight o'clock in the evening I would drive over in Mum's car to a farm in Enfield, where

I had to load a van with the afore-mentioned chips and then set off for London. The first night, getting to know the round, took me so long that I was late returning Mum's car, and she had to get the bus to work. However, I convinced her that the following night's work would take a lot less time, and she agreed to let me borrow the car again. This time the round went much better, and I returned her car in good time. The third night, just outside the West End, I spotted a girl hitch-hiking.

'Hop in' said I. 'What are you doing out this late?'

'Going to work'.

'Oh, what do you do?'

She gave me an old fashioned look.

'I'll give you three guesses'.

I looked over at her, took in her low cut blouse, very short skirt and high heels, and the penny dropped. I took her to the Wimpy Bar in Oxford Street, delivered the chips and continued my round. The next night, I saw her again, and again dropped her at the Wimpy Bar. I took their chips down into the basement, and as I started up the stairs, Tracy, my new friend, was standing at the top of the stairs with her feet wide apart, and hoisted her skirt up.

'Fancy one on the house?' she enquired coquettishly.

'No thanks' I said, 'I've got work to do'.

'Please yourself'.

As this job was only a stop-gap, I was spending an hour or two a day writing for interviews. One job that looked promising was as a sales representative selling to department stores in and around London. I applied, and two days later got a letter inviting me to Esher for an interview. I took the train and arrived at the offices of a company called Bellfax, situated very near Sandown Park Racecourse. I was interviewed by a man who asked to be called 'Colonel', and then by a man called Brunton-Green. As I prepared to leave, the Colonel said 'You've got my vote—you'll be hearing from us'. I did indeed hear from them with an offer to start work early the following year. I gave in my notice, and said goodbye to night shifts, and offers of freebies from ladies of the night.

Jim's brother David showed us a play he had written called 'A Bite of the Apple', a farce about God approaching the Celestial Patents Office with his invention, 'Man'. We all thought it a wonderful piece of work, and it was agreed that we would perform its world premiere at the Woking Drama Festival in October. I was honoured when David asked me to direct it, and as a thankyou, I cast the author as God! It deservedly won first prize in the new play category.

Christmas was not such a joyous occasion as it might have been; Ruth and I both realised that our marriage had not been made in heaven, I was again out of work, and we didn't possess a car of our own, let alone a house.

Chapter Twelve

Early in the New Year of 1971 I started work at Bellfax and became part of the national sales force. We all reported to Mr. Brunton-Green, the sales director, and I immediately got the feeling that this could, at last, turn out to be a job that might take me somewhere. Bellfax manufactured adhesive initials, to personalise luggage, wallets, handbags, etc., and also imported keyrings from the States, and my job was to sell them to department stores, gift shops and luggage shops. I was given the use of an Austin 1800—not the raciest of cars, but a very boring vehicle from the bad old days of British Leyland. It was, however, a car, and for the first time in ages, I didn't have to rely on other people for my transport. I took to the job like a duck to water, and it did indeed turn out to be the first step onto a career in selling to the gift trade, which in turn became very successful self-employment in the greetings card industry, many, many years later.

'The Colonel', as he liked to be known, was Colonel Edward Remington-Hobbs, DSO, and he was the company chairman. He was a fascinating character, a real ladies man and, unfortunately, a chain smoker. He had the rare distinction of being the sole survivor of an aeroplane crash in 1953, which killed, along with all the other passengers, his first wife. He married again in 1957, and then again in 1972. His third wife was the daughter of the American heiress, Lady Baillie, who had bought Leeds Castle in Kent. His time was spent at his mews house in London during the week, and at the Maiden's Tower in Leeds Castle at the weekend. He was very 'hands on', and if I had had a good week, he would load up his Daimler and deliver my orders to Harrods, Selfridges and other department stores where his face was well-known and invariably welcome. Many of my customers are no longer in existence—Bourne and Hollingsworth, Civil Service Stores, Swan and Edgar have all long since disappeared from the West End, but it was selling to them that honed my skills.

The Austin 1800 proved not to be particularly reliable, and, on one occasion when Ruth, Rebecca and I had driven into the country for a picnic, it tried to catch fire. Luckily, a one year old Rebecca spotted smoke emanating from the bonnet, and its attempt at self-immolation failed. I explained to the Colonel that I was not happy driving a car that might kill us all, and, in due course, it was replaced by a gleaming new white Ford Cortina. (Had I arrived, or what?)

Back in the world of the amateur theatre, our next production was 'A Severed Head' by Iris Murdoch, a complex marital comedy, which we performed at the Intimate Theatre in June. Ruth both directed and played the 'severed head', Honor Klein, with great panache. Although she and I were not blissfully happy, we enjoyed working together in the theatre, and she had cast me as her incestuous lover in the play. The next production, however, was to cause problems. Mike had by now started his own group, North London Productions, with the idea of taking plays on tour (to Littlehampton and beyond) and funding them himself, with the idea of turning his hobby into a profitable business. I must admit that I was not at all interested in the finances—I just wanted to act and direct.

This next production, which Mike had arranged to put on at the Windmill Theatre in Littlehampton, was 'Boeing Boeing', a farce by Marc Camoletti, and it was agreed that David and Pat were to play the male leads and I would direct. David had been introduced to us by Iris, a girl at Entens, another local drama group. He had been going through a rough time recently, having lost his job, his flat and his girlfriend all in the space of a week. However, he came recommended as a confident, reliable actor, with a good stage presence, and I had no hesitation in casting him and Pat as the joint leads. Pat's father and Justin had played together on the musical stage, which is how Pat got to know of us. He could sing and dance as well as act, and we all looked forward to a very professional show. We started rehearsals, but it immediately became apparent that David was having trouble learning his words. He did indeed possess charisma and a great stage presence, but he had one big drawback. He was a huge fan of Marlon Brando, who, as a method actor, regarded learning his words of secondary importance. As a film star, he had to be indulged, and many a director was forced to resort to ingenious methods to ensure that film fans eventually saw a performance that didn't appear that it had been made up on the spot. It is comparatively easy to overcome a problem like this on screen, but virtually impossible to overcome in the live theatre. It was even more important to know one's words when rehearsing a farce, as often it was a specific word or line that would trigger the next bit of business, which usually required split second timing. David promised to do his best to get to grips with his words and I approached the next rehearsal with high hopes. Unfortunately, very little had changed, and I was forced to tell David that, if he couldn't make a real effort, rehearsals were useless, because I couldn't get the continuity going that was required to make this show a success, and that I would have to replace him.

At the next rehearsal, he took one hundred and thirty two prompts (yes, you read that correctly) in the first scene, and I sacked him. As I already knew his words much better than he did, I decided to take over the part. That evening I told Ruth.

'I thought you were only going to direct it'.

'That was the plan', I said, 'but David is incapable of learning his words'.

'So you're going to leave me and your baby daughter again, are you?

'It will only be for a week' I said, lamely. A frosty silence ensued.

Rightly or wrongly, I stuck to my guns, and the company left for Littlehampton in August for a week's run. Pat and I had a good rapport on stage, Lilian, Francesca and Pat's wife, Susan were very glamorous air hostesses, and Chris D. played the maid to great comic effect. It turned out to be a very successful show, and David came down to see it, and had the decency to offer his congratulations backstage at the end of the run. Ruth was conspicuous by her absence.

After 'Boeing Boeing', I wisely took a small break from the amateur theatre, and concentrated on work.

Our adhesive initials and keyrings were selling well, and I was enjoying the work and getting better and better as a salesman. The break was short-lived, however. I had become an admirer of N. F. Simpson's work, and persuaded the Thalians to do 'The Form', a weird but very funny one act play. I directed it, with Christine, Jim and Kate in the cast. We entered it for two drama festivals (Brent and Enfield, if you must know), and we won third place at Enfield. Later in the month, we performed it at St. Saviours, but how many of the audience (or, indeed, the cast) understood it is anybody's guess.

Reading the local paper one day, I spotted an advertisement placed by the Samaritans, who were looking for actors and actresses to do role-play to assist in the training of their volunteers. I figured that this could be of mutual benefit; Kate and I would be able to hone our improvisational skills, while the trainees would learn about some of the problems they might come up against. Kate and I replied, and were invited to their offices in Wood Green. They asked us to improvise a scene with me playing a foul-mouthed, drunken wife beater, and Kate playing my wretched, helpless, hopeless wife. In front of four or five trainees and a group of senior Samaritans, Kate and I really went for it; I was screaming at her, threatening her with physical violence, and she responded, in character, by cowering, terrified, and bursting into tears. We later discovered, over coffee, that our performance had been so realistic that a number of trainee volunteers decided that they didn't want to become Samaritans after all!

Chapter Thirteen

One morning in 1972 I woke up and realised that I desperately wanted to play 'Alfie'. What had triggered this sudden urge after so many years, I know not, but it was suddenly very important that I get it out of my system. I went to Mike and told him that I wanted the Thalians to do the play, that I wanted to play the lead, and that I wanted him to find a director and be in overall charge of production. He looked searchingly at me.

'Bit of an ego trip, isn't it?'

'Yes' I said, 'but I think I could do it justice.'

He must have agreed with me, because, before I knew it, he had found a director and rehearsals were under way. With his various contacts within other drama groups, he had met a chap called Rex, who had studied at the Mountview Theatre Club; Mike had seen some of his work, and asked him if he would direct. Rex agreed, and turned out to be an inspired choice. The play was not an easy one to do, being, as it was, made up of twelve scenes, spread out over three acts, covering nine different locations. The scene shifters would be working overtime on this one. Another problem, mine alone, was learning the words. Alfie appeared in every single scene, and spent half his time addressing the audience directly, which meant he was not getting any cues thrown back at him. However, from the word go, it had been my baby, and I was determined to do the part justice. I wrote to the Paul Raymond organisation, and they kindly sent a couple of 'top shelf' magazines for the hospital scene, and Rael Brook kindly sent me half a dozen shirts, and, as a result, they were both were given a good acknowledgement in the programme. I decided that Alfie had more luxuriant hair than I did, (as did most men of my age) so I approached Wig Creations in Baker Street, who provided me with a lustrous dark brown wig. I found it very helpful to don the wig for rehearsals, and I began to inhabit the part. Rehearsals were a joy; I had worked with some of the cast before, (Chris D, Christine, Lilian, Mike, Eva) but a newcomer was Phil Davies, who played Humphrey, and Harry in the hospital scene, and his timing was superb.

Another newcomer was Annie, who had answered one of our adverts. She was a very attractive dark haired girl with a great figure, and had her own flat in Kensington; she would probably be regarded today as 'posh totty'. I warmed to her immediately, and suggested that she and I indulge in some extra-curricular rehearsals (nudge, nudge, wink, wink). She declined my offer, saying she didn't think that would be necessary. The following evening, however, she rang to say she had changed her mind, and could she come round to Rockville later that evening? She duly turned up, and within half an hour we were rehearsing on the rug in front of the fire. What we rehearsed never actually appeared in the play, but our scenes together were all the better for it.

We did two performances in July at the Intimate Theatre, then took the show to Littlehampton in August. The language proved a little too much for some of the senior citizens, however, who got up and walked out. (It was a good job they hadn't seen the Mountview Theatre production that Christine and I had attended during our rehearsals; Alfie's constant 'bleedin' this' and 'bleedin' that' had become 'fuckin' this' and 'fuckin' that'. As well as this, in the opening scene, Siddie had fondly caressed Alfie's crotch. Christine turned to me and said 'Well, I'm certainly not doing THAT!') Our production, however, was true to the script, and was generally agreed to have been a success, (and to my mind superior to the Mountview Theatre Club production) helped in no small way by Rex's choice of music—Dionne Warwick singing 'A House is not a Home', 'The look of Love' and, of course, 'Alfie' (in preference to Cilla Black's version). My contribution to the music was to suggest 'Sweet Talkin' Guy' by The Chiffons, which seemed to me to encapsulate Alfie to perfection. The play is as fresh and fascinating now as I write this, because, unbeknown to me at the time, Rex had recorded the Saturday night performance at the Intimate Theatre. One particularly fond memory from that performance is the three line joke concerning Ruby: 'She's 'ad two husbands'—pause—'both dead'—pause—'an' I've a bleedin' good idea what they died of, an' all!'—laugh. On this particular night it went as follows: 'She's 'ad two husbands'—pause—'both dead'—big laugh, which I didn't expect, so I waited and waited for the laugh to fade, and then hit them with the punchline, which got an even bigger laugh. A reminder of how different, and how much more rewarding, performing on stage was as opposed to filming.

Whether or not it was as a result of my performance, I was invited to join the Mountview Theatre Club to appear in their production of 'Close the Coalhouse Door', a very funny, left wing slant on the miners' strike. It was an ensemble production, involving a lot of lusty (if tuneless) singing, and it went down very well. I had received a 'break a leg' telegram from Annie, who would later direct Shirley and me in the filthy farce 'What the Butler Saw' by Joe Orton. To my great pleasure and satisfaction, I received a charming letter from Dennis Rodbert offering me Honorary Membership.

Jenny and her Mum, Eva, were going through an awkward period, and were spending a lot of time arguing. One evening, Jenny rang me in tears, asking if she could come and stay at Rockville for a while. I agreed. David and Mike were already staying there regularly, and Jenny and David were to become regular fixtures.

Kay had been increasingly frustrated and unhappy with her career in the police and, after some serious soul searching, decided she was going to become a nun. We were what could be perceived as a dysfunctional family, I had never, ever, seen Dad show the slightest sign of affection to Mum, nor, indeed, to Kay and me; Mum and Dad would regularly go to the pictures, but while Dad went to the Odeon, Mum would go to the Gaumont, or vice versa. Although I am sure Mum loved us, she had great difficulty in showing her emotions, and Mum and Dad's attitude obviously affected Kay quite adversely. She left to go to Tymawr, a convent in Wales near Monmouth, and was to stay there for the next ten years. She had 'found God', and regarded Dad and me as heathens. He once told me that if he were to belong to any religious group, it would be the Incas, because they worshipped the sun, which gave them heat and light. My own feelings, which had begun as hesitant agnostic, were slowly but resolutely becoming atheistic. I was an iconoclast, and perhaps it was the polarity of our opinions and beliefs that ensured that Kay and I would endure a tempestuous relationship throughout our lives.

In September, Mike decided to take 'The Caretaker', by Harold Pinter abroad to tour France, but Tom, one of the cast, was arrested at Dover for a passport irregularity. Mike and Tim got the boat to Calais, where all their scenery was impounded! Frantic phone calls to Ruth, asking for her father (a barrister) to help out, eventually ensured that Tom was released, and the group arrived in Paris for their first performance with but two hours to spare. The tour continued successfully, and Mike managed to make a profit.

I woke up one morning in October 1973 with another 'must do'—this time it had nothing to do with the theatre, but I decided I had to buy Rockville. I told Dad, who looked at me as though I had completely lost the plot. When Aunt Floss heard, she immediately sent me a cheque for £500, and my fund was underway. It was agreed that, if I could raise the money (which Dad thought highly unlikely), I could buy the house for £14,000, slightly below the market value. Dad was about to retire, and he and Mum were going to Northampton, to be near Floss, who had moved there with her husband from South London.

On 25th November Laurence Harvey died of cancer, aged forty five.

Work continued to go well at Bellfax and the company moved from Esher to new purpose-built premises in the Barwell Trading Estate, just up the road from Chessington Zoo, as it was then, Chessington World of Adventures as it is now. The theatre had now taken a back seat as far as I was concerned and I was aware that a worthwhile career in selling beckoned. I was seeing Jenny and Kate on a regular basis, and early in December had an interesting evening. Kate and I had arranged to meet for a drink in Muswell Hill, and she agreed to come back to Rockville for a spot of hanky-panky. We were in separate cars, and I suggested she park her car out of sight in Harcourt Road. She did, and we repaired to the upstairs back bedroom. At about ten o'clock, we heard the front door opening, and Mike and Tommy came up the stairs, and went into the lounge. This understandably quenched our ardour somewhat, and I got up and went in to the lounge to apologise to Mike and Tommy that I couldn't join them because I was entertaining a young lady. On the way back to the bedroom, I spotted the wide brimmed hat that Jenny had bought a couple of weeks earlier; I took it to Kate, who was now dressed, and she tip-toed down the stairs wearing Jenny's hat. She successfully departed without Tommy discovering that it was his wife I had been with.

The following weekend, I went down to Tymawr to see Kay in February 1974. She seemed happy, but the regime at the convent was a fairly harsh one. The nuns were self-sufficient, driving a tractor, tending cattle and growing their own fruit and vegetables, but apparently spent most of their time in prayer and silent meditation.

In April, the Eurovision Song Contest was set alight by a new group from Sweden called Abba. The two girls, Agnetha and Anni-Frid, looked sensational, had beautiful voices and wore very sexy outfits—I immediately fell in love with both of them. They were runaway winners with 'Waterloo', which was the first of their nine number one hits.

Mike was more and more involved with North London Productions, and presented 'The Taming of the Shrew', 'The Boyfriend', 'Hay Fever' and 'The Owl and the Pussycat' during the year. Jim and Sheila got married in June, and in July, Tommy, Kate, David, Christy, Jill and I went on holiday to Yugoslavia (as it was then). The sun was fierce, but this didn't stop David and me from going to a nudist beach one morning. We came to the conclusion that swimming naked in the sea was very exhilarating, and that most girls looked a lot sexier with a swimming costume on. The holiday was made memorable by 'The Slivovitz Incident'—Tommy and I got drunk on the stuff one evening, and Tommy made off with Jill while I made out with Kate. The next morning, Tommy and Jill arrived at the breakfast table first, followed soon after by Kate and me. The situation was potentially embarrassing for all four of us, but any problem was quickly defused after Tommy and I had a drink of water. This had the same effect as having a slug of slivovitz, and we both burst into hysterical laughter. The other couples in the room were totally perplexed by now, having been used to seeing Tommy arriving for meals with Kate, and me with Jill. We were now with the wrong partners and apparently helpless with drunken hilarity at nine o'clock in the morning. David and Christy then arrived, wondering what the hell was going on.

Although we all thoroughly enjoyed ourselves, there were issues with the quality of our rooms, the service, and a dangerous rocky area on the beach area that had not been mentioned in the brochure. Tommy called a meeting of the six of us, and showed us the draft of a letter he proposed to send to British Airtours, our tour operators. We all agreed that the letter should be sent, seeking compensation for our grievances.

Back home, we received a reply refusing our claim for compensation, so it was agreed that we would take them to the small claims court.

I had now got a mortgage in place (at an interest rate of 15%!) and in September we exchanged contracts on Rockville, and my foot was now, at long last, on the first rung of the property ladder.

In October, Miriam, who by now had separated from Reg, held a party at her new house in Paddock Wood. Bruce and I drove down together, and apparently caused quite an impression amongst the local girls, who regarded us as 'London Lads' and therefore highly desirable. We enjoyed ourselves immensely, and drove back the following morning, each sporting a wide grin.

Mark and Christine had decided to employ an au-pair, and that is how I met Isabella, a randy Spanish lass. I dallied with her now and again, as did many others, and later discovered that she had been voted the most popular au-pair in North London (at least, I think popular was the adjective!).

Tommy.	'My dad's got two willies'.
Bertie.	'Don't be silly—nobody's got two willies'.
Tommy.	'Well, my Dad has—he's got a little one he pees with, and a big one the au-pair cleans her teeth with'.

In November, we took British Airtours to court. When the magistrate asked if the plaintiffs were present, and all six of us stood up, his face was a picture. He listened to the evidence, and then the chap representing the tour operators made us an offer of £90 per person. We asked for time to consider, and went over the road to think about it. Tommy said 'Who thinks we should accept?' and five hands, including his, went up. 'I think we should hold out for more' said I, but I was out-voted, and I accepted the majority decision. I still think we should not have accepted their first offer, and am convinced that this victory over British Airtours set the scene for my interest in future litigation.

Ruth, just after our wedding.

Rehearsing...

...for Alfie.

Justin, Francesca, Diana Churchill and a grinning ape after the Saturday performance of 'Murder'. I was mercifully omitted from the photo that appeared in the local press.

With Kate in Yugoslavia.

With Rebecca on the way to Bristol to see John and Sandra.

With Rebecca at 77 Dartmouth Park Hill.

After Christmas spent partly at Rockville, and partly at Mum and Dad's new bungalow in Northampton, Tommy, Kate, Jill and I decided to spend our compensation on a trip to see the New Year (1975) in in Majorca. Waiting in the queue to board the plane, we couldn't help noticing a Rolls Royce with the number plate FAL 1 on the runway. Once on board, Freddie Laker, for it was indeed he, introduced himself to us all, and, to the audible groans of the air hostesses, invited everybody to inspect the flight deck. Thankyou, Freddie, for that, and for Skytrain, and for setting the scene for Richard Branson, Michael Ryan and Stelios Haji-Ioannou to follow suit in later years.

Two young couples decided to go on a week's holiday, and booked a cottage in the West Country. On their second morning there, the two husbands are sitting at the breakfast table.

First Bloke.   'Your wife's a dirty cow, isn't she?'
Second Bloke (bristling). 'What do you mean'.
First Bloke.   'Well, I got up in the middle of the night to have a piss in the sink, and it was full of dirty dishes!'

Parties at Rockville were becoming a regular feature of North London life, and a crowd of us would often repair there after a rehearsal or a show. One particularly surreal party, attended by, amongst others, Mike, Lilian, David, Jenny, Kate, Tommy, Mark, Christine, Jim and Sheila involved, not surprisingly, a lot of smoking, drinking and loud music. Somebody put 'Crocodile Rock' by Elton John on the record player (no such thing as an iPod in those days) and I found myself dancing with Tommy! We were whirling round the room, dancing like demented dervishes (sorry, another attack of the alliteratives . . . well, it has been a while) when I thought to myself, hang on a minute, you're having an affair with the wife and dancing with the husband . . . I ended the evening, however, having a slow dance with Jenny, which seemed a much more heterosexual thing to do. Another party, even more surreal, was at Terry and Sue's house, and again involved Kate and Tommy. I found Don Maclean's 'American Pie' impossible to sit still to, and asked Kate for a dance. One dance became four or five, and I eventually sat down, exhausted. Guests subsequently left or went upstairs to bed. Later, finding myself alone, I went upstairs in search of a bed, and, opening one bedroom door, was surprised to see Kate in bed alone, with Tommy nowhere to be seen. I stripped off and jumped in beside her, but she wanted nothing to do with me, and turned over with her back to me. I drifted off to sleep, and awoke the following morning with the feel of warm flesh next to me. I was about to say something witty when the warm flesh, in the shape of Tommy, got up, stared enigmatically at me, and left the room.

Sales of keyrings and initials continued to climb and I was getting genuine satisfaction from the job. I had built up a good relationship with my customers, particularly Harrods and Selfridges, and was getting a real buzz from opening new accounts, and my enthusiasm for, and my success in, my work had not gone unnoticed. My relationship with Ruth, however, was not cordial, but I did my best to have Rebecca over to Rockville every weekend. I would collect her from Dartmouth Park Hill on a Friday evening, and we would sometimes deliver orders I had taken during the week to department stores in the West End on Saturday morning. I tried to keep Saturday evenings free for her, and would cook Sunday lunch before returning her to Dartmouth Park Hill on Sunday evening. Unfortunately, her mother and grandparents were often still drinking in the Lord Palmerston until well gone eleven o'clock, and returning Rebecca to the bosom of her mother's family was sometimes not as good natured as it might have been.

Question. What do I have in common with Frank Sinatra and Tom Cruise?

Answer. All three of us have played Nathan Detroit in 'Guys and Dolls'. Mike and Pat had set up another company called Normandy Productions, and had decided to present 'Guys and Dolls' as their first production. I had been cast for my acting ability rather than my singing ability, but I went at it with great enthusiasm, and we performed the show for three nights at the Intimate Theatre. This would be my last appearance on stage, and I now directed all my energies to work (well, most of them, anyway). This decision would change the course of my life.

Back at Bellfax, Mr Brunton-Green called me in to his office one morning. 'Well, Tony, the Colonel and I would like to say that we think you are doing a good job, and we are delighted with the progress you are making. As a result of this, we have decided to give you some help. We have taken on a young lady as a merchandiser to assist you with your key accounts in London. She is a seventeen year old blue eyed blonde who looks like Britt Ekland, and I am warning you now to keep your hands off her'. As my hands were already more than full, I nodded in agreement. 'Her name is Angela Hammond-Gabbitas, she starts next week, and I am expecting you to show her the ropes'. Angela started on £30 per week plus 1% commission.

I got a call on Friday to say that she would be waiting outside the Piccadilly Hotel at 10 o'clock the following Wednesday morning. I set off at eight forty five to meet, although I didn't know it then, my future wife. She was as unimpressed with me as I was with her. She saw me as an old fart, and I saw her as a possible disruption to my ordered and well-regulated work routine. It soon dawned on me, however, that if she were to prove capable of looking after my customers, the way might be open for me to extend and expand my areas of activity. This is indeed what happened, and I soon found myself trouble-shooting in new areas. Angela turned out to be a willing learner and a more than capable merchandiser and became more and more involved with my key accounts.

On 17th July, I helped her celebrate her eighteenth birthday, and bought her a pack of twenty No 6 cigarettes and a Bic lighter as her present (I knew the way to a girl's heart!).

In August, we exhibited at the Earls Court Gift Fair, and it occurred to me that although Angela had a steady boyfriend, Mick, and I had my girlfriends, we were getting to like each other and became friends.

Lilian went to see Kate about a dress she wanted altering, and Kate noticed a swelling under Lilian's armpit.

'You should have that looked at' said Kate. Lilian did, and it was diagnosed as cancer.

On 23rd December we all celebrated with Christmas lunch at the office. A slightly inebriated Angela and I went up to Selfridges to do some Christmas shopping, and we later dallied for a while in the car park.

1976 started with David joining us as a sales representative for the Home Counties and preparations for the Spring Fair at the N E C in Birmingham. We left on Friday 30th January and spent the whole week there. Angela was now well into her stride, doing increasingly good business in and around London, and was a hard working professional on the stand. One evening, after a heavy snowfall, Angela and I had great fun skidding around the hotel car park, and later had even more fun in my room; the friendship was progressing!

I had now been promoted to Area Manager, which involved travelling further afield, and I left on Sunday 15th. February for four days in York. On my return, to celebrate my promotion, I had some new visiting cards printed, with the legend *'A. E. R. Shelton M. Inst. S. M.'* I had joined the Institute of Sales Management, and thought it impressive to have letters after my name (well, I was impressed).

Jill had some time ago met a chap called Blair, who turned out to be the love of her life, and they decided to tie the knot. David, Tommy, Mike and I and sundry others joined up to celebrate Blair's stag night in the West End. We all managed to sober up in time for the wedding at Caxton Hall on the Saturday, where I was delighted to be best man. Blair and I wore matching green suits, and I had my hair dyed to hide the increasing onslaught of grey. I escorted Kate to the celebrations, but behaved abominably towards her. One of the guests, a friend of Blair's, was a very attractive girl called Tinch (where the hell did she get that name from?) and, true to form, the sap started to rise. At the end of the evening, I gave Kate my car keys, said goodnight, and went back with Tinch to her place, where I stayed the night. It was a long walk home the following morning, and Kate was understandably upset when I saw her next, but, being the girl she was, she forgave me.

Later that month, I was in Birmingham, interviewing for the post of Sales Rep. for the West Midlands, and at the end of the month I was in Bournemouth with our South West rep, Terry. April was hectic, spending time with the sales force, agreeing targets, organising in-store promotions, and helping to ensure the smooth running of the sales office. In May, I was in Leeds, interviewing for a sales rep. in the North West. I was staying in the Dragonara, and on returning one evening after dinner, spotted a white Rolls-Royce, number plate MB 1, parked outside. Scattered all over the car were various eight-track cartridges, all by Max Bygraves. (Apparently, he had turned down an offer of £15,000 for the plate from Mercedes Benz).

On Sunday 16th May, I drove up to Northampton to see Mum and Dad. Mum had lost weight and looked very frail, and I learnt that the cancer had returned, this time in her stomach. Dad was looking after her, but the strain was making him look haggard, and he confided that Mum had considered committing suicide. It must have been a miserable existence for both of them, not helped by the fact that Dad had not wanted to live in Northampton; Mum had wanted to be near Floss, whose husband had died, and Dad had agreed in order to keep Mum happy.

Later that month, I was promoted to Sales Manager, and Pauline, one of the girls in the office, became my secretary. This time, the boss/secretary relationship would be a purely business one; Pauline was very efficient and, in time, became an intuitive and reliable organiser of my diary (my business diary, that is). One morning, however, she confided in me that the previous evening she had received a phone call from a heavy breather who was keen to discover what colour knickers she was wearing. That evening, I phoned her at home, and enquired, in my most suggestive tone, what colour ribbon she had in her typewriter. She was about to slam the phone down in disgust, when she realised who it was, and collapsed in helpless laughter. Meanwhile, Angela was proving to be a gifted saleswoman and was promoted to London Sales

Rep, and was bringing in more and more business from London; Mr. Brunton-Green and the Colonel agreed with me that she should not have to continue using public transport, and the company presented her with a Mini; not a new one, but one which had been used as a runabout for the staff at Leeds Castle; in fact Angela used to comment that it ran on a mixture of oil and water and was a rust heap! She was, however, delighted to be presented with a company car at such a young age.

Bruce had bought a flat in Ladbroke Grove, but because of his peripatetic nature, was not often there; he was happy for me to stay there whenever I wanted, and I stayed there now and again if I had an early start in London the following morning. One night I dreamt of Jenny. She had been a regular at Hatchetts discotheque, and had wanted to take me there. I was not a fan of discotheques, finding that the combination of dim lighting, ear-splitting music and eye-watering prices were not exactly my cup of tea; however, one night, to please her, I agreed to tag along. We drove up to Piccadilly and spent an hour inside before my patience ran out. We had smuggled in a bottle of spirits, so that I only had to buy us one round of drinks. We went back to the car, both a little over the limit, and drove off. Within fifty yards or so, a policeman stepped out into the road with his hand up. I was in no mood to be stopped, and kept my foot on the throttle. The policeman jumped out of the way, and we drove back to Rockville. Sometimes, my dreams worried me . . .

In June, after seeing Kay on the 13th, it was up to Leeds once again. Our interviews had proved successful, and we took on Noreen as our rep. in the North East, and Joan as our rep in the North West. I was there for three days to show Noreen the ropes; from there I went up to Newcastle, then back down to Harrogate for the Gift Fair. My social life had slowed down somewhat, my acting was non-existent, but my career was going from strength to strength. I was now earning a decent salary, plus commission and bonus, and an expense account to boot. Work was going well, Angela and I were developing a rapport which exceeded normal business boundaries, sales were improving all the time, and I was enjoying the pressure and responsibility of running a sales force.

The white Cortina was now beginning to show signs of age, and a replacement car was ordered. I was still only allowed a Cortina, but this time it was the two litre version in the very latest colour—wait for it—'Sahara Beige'!

Things were improving on all fronts with Angela, and one evening, after a good day's work, we went to Queensway for a Chinese meal, then spent the night together at Bruce's flat. Later that week, Angela and

Mick came up to Rockville for a party—Mick was not impressed, and was beginning to suspect that all was not tickety-boo between him and Angela. Life was becoming complicated for her, now having two men in her life.

In September, I went up to Manchester to spend two or three days with our agent, Frank. He was the only member of the sales force who was self-employed, and a real character. He regarded himself, not without reason, as a hard man. He had spent his youth in the Navy, and was now a grizzled, chain-smoking, hard drinking, successful salesman. When I first became Sales Manager, I was concerned that I would not be able to win his confidence—what would a young, relatively inexperienced Southern softie like me be able to teach him? We spent the days visiting his customers, and the evenings at his club, eating, drinking, smoking and gambling. We developed a mutual respect for one another, and, underneath his hard man exterior, I realised there lurked a heart of gold.

The Mini was now falling apart, and Bellfax delighted Angela by replacing it with a brand new white Ford Escort Popular Plus. Well deserved.

In October, I went up to see Mum and Dad. Mum was now terminally ill, and Kay had been granted a dispensation from the convent to be with her. Mum had now shrunk to the size of not much larger than a baby, and was a pale yellow colour. She asked me if we could take her out in her wheelchair, and I got the impression she had already asked Dad, and for some reason he had refused. We wrapped her up well, and I pushed her round the area for half an hour, and we returned with her sporting a wan smile. That was to be my final memory of her—she died later in the month—a blessed relief for Dad and Kay, who had shouldered the enormous burden of nursing her, and for Mum, whose later life had been riddled with both physical and mental illness. Angela lost her grandfather in the same month.

We had started doing business last year with a shop in Malta, and I suggested to Mr. Brunton-Green that I combine a winter break with a visit to our customer, and would Bellfax split the bill with me? He agreed, and when I asked Dad, now living alone, if he would like to come with me, he jumped at the chance.

A couple of days later, Bruce phoned to say he had a car that might interest me, and would I like to pop over to his house in Hammersmith to give it the once-over? I did so, and was introduced to 'The Beast'. 'The Beast' was a Daimler Double Six in dark blue, with lashings of chrome, grey leather upholstery and a magnificent 5.3 litre Jaguar V12 engine under the bonnet.

'It can get from here to Heathrow in eight minutes' said Bruce.

'Prove it' said I.

Seven minutes, fifty eight seconds later we arrived at Heathrow. However, as Bruce's dinner was ready, we decided against flying off anywhere, and drove back to Hammersmith at a slightly (but only slightly) more leisurely pace.

'What does it do to the gallon' said I.

'Don't ask' said Bruce.

I figured if Bellfax would pay me a car allowance instead of providing me with a car, I could afford to run it. I asked Bruce if I could borrow it for a day to have it checked out at a Jaguar/Daimler garage in Leatherhead. (The colonel had his car serviced there, and introduced me to the service manager, who gave the car a clean bill of health.)

'How much do you want for it' said I.

'Two thousand five hundred' said Bruce.

'I'll give you two thousand, two hundred and fifty' said I.

'Done' said Bruce.

I was about to embark on a love affair that would last many years.

Because Angela was doing such a good job, we were intent on bolstering the sales force in London, and I was interviewing girls to take on the post of merchandiser for Angela in the West End. One girl that particularly impressed me, and subsequently got the job, was Marion, who was nicely spoken and had an excellent CV. The fact that she was blonde, had a nice smile, a lovely figure and looked like Angela had nothing to do with it.

Chapter Fourteen

On 23rd January 1977, Dad and I flew off to Malta, to stay in the Hilton at St. Juliens Bay. The next morning, my thirty seventh birthday, we caught a bus into Valetta so that I could call on our customer. Whilst I was chatting to him we were aware of a disturbance just up the road. I asked him what was going on, and he explained that a pimp was keeping some of his stroppy girls in line. He gave me an order for key-rings, and I rejoined Dad to explore Valetta. That evening, after dinner, we went to the bar for a drink, but after only one, he decided to go to bed. I stayed for another drink, and spotted a very attractive redhead sitting on her own. I offered to buy her a drink, and she accepted. We got chatting, and I told her about the disturbance earlier in the say. She smiled. I asked her what she was doing on her own in the bar, and she told me she was one of the girls I had heard earlier.

'And what do you charge for your services?' I asked.

'Ten pounds' she said, 'or twenty to stay the night'.

I finished my drink and stood up.

'I've never paid for it' I said, 'and I'm not going to start now. I bid you goodnight'. (Pretentious git.)

Dad and I spent the rest of our time there enjoying the weather, and on our last night we decided to go next door to the Dragonara Casino. We spent a couple of hours playing blackjack, and then Dad ran out of money. I lent him some more, and we played for another hour. By now, we had both spent as much as we had intended, and got up to leave. On the way out, I discovered that I still had a fifty pence piece in my pocket, and, as a last insouciant gesture I threw it down onto the roulette table. Imagine my face when the number came up at 35 to 1, and I walked out after three and a half hours with a profit. Dad couldn't really believe it, and looked at me with what was almost respect.

Dad and I returned on Sunday 30th, and Marion started the following day. I was immediately involved with preparations for the Spring Fair, which always started on the first Sunday in February. Because of this, I was rarely in London for Rebecca's birthday, but this year was an exception, and we spent a nice evening together celebrating her seventh birthday. I left for Birmingham on Friday to set up the stand, and worked all day Saturday. After a good meal in the evening, Angela coaxed me back to her room for a coffee. During the week, I got a cold and felt lousy. Angela insisted on coming to my room to play nurse.

The Spring Fair was a resounding success, and back in London, Angela and I went out for dinner. Later, back at Rockville, I fell asleep and had a vivid and most memorable dream. Angela and I were returning from Birmingham down the M1 and the Beast was begging to be let off its leash. As the traffic thinned, and I could see a clear road ahead, I gave it some welly: 80, 90, 100, 110, 120, 130—then, with the speedo registering 138 mph the traffic in front of us suddenly seemed to be coming towards us at a hell of a lick, and I backed off. I glanced across at Angela, who had an expression of absolute terror on her face.

Upon our return, our work was cut out following up all the leads we had generated. I spent time with Angela and Marion, showing Marion the ropes in London. However, this could hardly be described as hard work, involving, as it did, spending time in the company of two beautiful young blondes. Talking of beautiful young blondes (as one does . . . frequently . . .) Bellfax had recently introduced a range of funky plastic key fobs, and

I asked Jenny if she would be interested in modelling them by doing a fashion shoot in the West End. She readily agreed, and one morning we drove to Carnaby Street. Jenny was dressed in a lime green blouse, crushed velvet hot pants and knee high white boots. I was taking photos of her outside a trendy boutique, when one of the sales girls came out. I persuaded her to adorn herself, as Jenny had, with key fobs, and took more photos. I then decided some more shots in Oxford Street would be a good idea, and stopped the traffic momentarily to get Jenny to pose in the middle of the road. (an arrestable offence these days, I shouldn't wonder).

After a particularly good week, thanks to Angela and Marion, Friday evening found a crowd of us at the Fox and Hounds. After a couple of drinks, Angela and I slunk off in the Beast, and parked down a country lane. We enjoyed a cuddle in the back, but when it was time to leave, we realised that the car was stuck in the mud and slowly sliding down a river bank. I rang the AA, who arrived to tow us out. The patrolman could not resist giving Angela the once-over, and me a knowing smile.

The Daimler was now my regular form of transport, and I was enjoying it immensely. It was supremely comfortable, and a dream at speed. It was one of the few cars that could out accelerate a Rolls-Royce and yet at 70 mph was quieter than a Rolls. It was not so happy in traffic jams, though; as the temperature gauge went up, steam would emanate from the wheel arches; it was as though the car was hissing at me 'I want to be let off the leash'. At the end of March, Angela and Marion were working London together, and I drove up to Leeds (letting the Beast off the leash) for two days with Noreen, then on to Manchester for a couple of days with Frank.

Marion was turning out to be every bit as good as I thought she would, and Angela was being groomed to spend more time outside London. She and I, having developed respect for one another, were now taking the relationship into new areas, and were continuing to spend extra-curricular time with one another. I, in the meantime, enjoyed my first visit to Scotland, via the shuttle from Heathrow, to spend time with our new agent.

Later that month I spent time with David in Norwich, Ipswich and Romford, and at the end of the month was in Nottingham with our rep Peter, followed by two days in Wetherby with Joan. I was back up there again in May, followed by three days in Newcastle. I was beginning to forget what my bed in Rockville was like. One weekend that was spent at home, however, turned out to be a bit traumatic. Angela and I had collected Rebecca from Dartmouth Park Hill, and were driving her through Crouch End, when a woman driver pulled out of a side street and struck us amidships. Although we hadn't been hurt, it had frightened Rebecca, and had not done my car much good. I took Rebecca back home the following evening, and drove the damaged Daimler down to Leatherhead for repairs.

Our rep in the South West, Terry, had decided to move on. It was a wise decision, because his sales were declining, and he decided to jump before he was pushed. He was replaced by a tall, good looking aristocratic fellow called Robin, and I planned a trip with him to introduce him to some of our key accounts. The Daimler was not going to be ready in time, so I hired a very racy powder blue Triumph TR7. We set off on Sunday 22nd. May for the Holiday Inn in Plymouth, to be ready for an early start on Monday morning. We had a very successful three days, and returned from a highly enjoyable trip (in more ways than one) and I took the TR7 back, which had been thoroughly enjoyable, and collected a pristine Daimler.

By now, poor Lilian was in a bad way, and I went to visit her in the Royal Free Hospital in Hampstead. She had been with Mike to Germany for some revolutionary treatment, which had been unsuccessful, and was now receiving chemotherapy. She had lost all her hair; was wearing a wig, but looked completely drained and spoke in a tired, resigned way. She had been an active member of the Thalians; she had directed, been very good as an air hostess in 'Boeing Boeing' and even better as the doctor in 'Alfie', and had been enjoyable company offstage.

At the end of June, I again flew up to Edinburgh for a very successful meeting with the John Menzies buyer, and in July we started preparations for the Harrogate Fair. It was decided that, in order to save money, the stand and stock would be taken up in three cars rather than hiring a van. Peter and Joan were summoned down to Chessington, and we loaded their Sierras and the Daimler. Peter and Joan were despatched, and I set off after them half an hour later. After an hour and a half, I still had not caught up with them, so I decided to put the hammer down. Going north up a quiet M1, I pushed the speed up to 90, then 100, then 110, then 120. It was at this speed that the front offside tyre exploded. The steering wheel was momentarily wrenched out of my hands, and the car slammed into the central reservation before bouncing off. I had the presence of mind not to brake, and managed to steer the car gently onto the hard shoulder where we came to rest. The three cars I had overtaken not two minutes ago sailed past without bothering to stop. I called the AA, and they arrived within half an hour, but they needed to tow the car to the nearest garage to sort things out. In the meantime, I rang Bellfax to let them know what had happened, and they promised to try and make contact with Peter or Joan to arrange for us to meet up in Leeds.

I went for a coffee, and got chatting to the bloke at the next table. When he heard my story, he offered me a lift into Leeds. On the way there, he told me that his wife had gone to her mother's for a couple of days, and that he was looking forward to spending some time with his mistress (definition of a mistress—something in between a mister and a mattress). We pulled up outside a hotel in Leeds city centre, and five minutes later his mistress arrived. She was one of the ugliest women I had ever seen, with a face like a horse. I wondered what his wife must look like if this was his idea of enjoying a bit on the side. After thanking him for the lift, I rang Bellfax again, and learnt that Joan would meet me within the hour and run me back down to the car, which should, by then, have been repaired.

She did, it was, and we continued our journey to Harrogate at a more respectable pace.

On 16th August, at Graceland, Elvis died, aged forty two—an ignominious end to what had been a life enhancing career. Lilian died at the end of September, aged thirty two, and the Thalians turned out en masse to her cremation early in October.

Later that month, David left Bellfax, and Bruce was working at Rank Xerox. It would not be long before he suggested to Angela that she could earn much more money there than at Bellfax. She, however, was loving her job, enjoying working with me, and decided to stick with the status quo. How delighted she was to learn, therefore, that the company had decided, once more, to upgrade her company car—this time to a very sexy, low-slung 2.0 Ford Capri in silver, with a black vinyl roof.

In November, I was up to Wetherby again to see Joan. She and I got on very well, and I felt she was doing a good job on our behalf. Although I was staying at the Wetherby Turnpike, we went back to her house one evening after dinner for a drink. We ended up in her front room, kissing and cuddling on the sofa while her husband was upstairs in bed. What on earth we thought we were playing at, I know not. She declined my offer to come back to the hotel, which was probably very sensible. Away from her house and her husband, she might have let go completely and regretted it later.

On Christmas Eve Angela came up to Rockville, and after a couple of games of chess, we went out for dinner with Jill, Blair, Kate, and Bruce and his wife. Angela and I spent the night at Rockville, and she drove back to Epsom the following morning to spend Christmas with her family and Mick.

Chapter Fifteen

1978 started with my first visit to the Torquay Gift Show in January, followed by the Spring Fair at the N E C. Angela had now moved into Rockville, and her parents had bought a flat in Benidorm, and it was agreed that Bruce and I would spend a week there together in April, then he would fly home, and Angela would come out to join me. The fact that Angela and I had booked a holiday for the same week had not gone un-noticed at the office, and Mrs. Dorey, in the accounts department, said as much. 'Yes', I said, 'what a coincidence'. One cold day, I was sunbathing on the balcony. Bruce took one look at me and said 'I don't want to worry you, but you're not turning brown, you're turning blue'. He decided to leave after five days. I then had two days on my own before collecting Angela from the airport, and we spent a blissful week together, the weather now glorious.

In June I spent three lovely days in Dublin with our Irish agent—Guinness really did taste better there.

At the end of the month, Suzie and Christine joined us, and the team of Angela, Marion, Noreen, Joan, Suzie and Chris became collectively known as 'Tony's Angels'.

In July, the team and I were off to Harrogate, and, after another successful show, we returned in time to celebrate Angela's 21st birthday at the Fox and Hounds with a party with all her family and friends.

Uncle Albert died at the end of September. I had not had much to do with him over the years, but he was a character, and completely different from Dad. In fact, the family were all agreed that I should have been the extrovert Uncle Albert's son, and cousin Michael should have been the introvert Dad's son.

Angela and I spent a very pleasant Christmas at Rockville and drove up to see Dad on Boxing Day.

Chapter Sixteen

1979 started with the Colonel and Mr. Brunton-Green calling me into the Colonel's office to announce that they were promoting Angela to Key Accounts Executive, and as a result of my work over the years, they were promoting me to Sales Director. Wow! Me—a company director. My first job as Sales Director was to arrange a Sales Conference. A local motel was booked, the sales force were summoned, and we had a good dinner followed by drinks in the bar. We eventually got to bed, feeling very mellow, and the next morning at Bellfax, I realised that I had mislaid the key to the sales office, where the conference was to be held. I asked Joan to go back to the motel to see if I had left them there. I had, and Joan returned just in time for me to unlock the office before the Colonel arrived. The conference went very well; business was at an all-time high, we outlined our plans for the Spring Fair, and my promotion was announced.

On Friday 2nd February we departed for Birmingham, meaning that yet again I had to miss Rebecca's birthday. We had our best ever show, taking orders to the value of £25,000. While I flew up to Scotland again for a couple of days, Angela and Suzie went to the flat in Benidorm for a week. Upon my return, however, I was called into a meeting with the other directors and our accountants. We learnt, to our horror, that our best selling key ring, the A79, was being sold at less than it cost us! We had previously been importing it from our American supplier, but it had been decided to make it ourselves in the U.K. The sums had not been done correctly, and we were making a loss on every one we sold. We had returned from the trade show thinking how well we had done, with sales of the A79, in particular, having been exceptional, but, the sums not having been done, the triumph turned out to be a disaster. The one bright spot was that our stick-on initials had also sold well, at a good profit, but they only represented less than 10% of our overall sales. I could see the writing on the wall, and pondered my next move. Angela decided to take Bruce's advice, and started with Rank Xerox, where she forged a very successful, and very lucrative, career. Working together at Bellfax had become extremely complicated as our relationship was kept quiet from everybody. There was a lot that was suspected but not proven. Whereas people could have accused me of favouritism, nothing was further from the truth, I worked Angela harder and expected more of her because of our relationship. Angela also was dissatisfied with travelling away so much. She was often away when I was in the office or she was in the office and I was away, hence we weren't seeing that much of each other.

With Jenny in the kitchen at Rockville.

A rose between two thorns – with Jill and Blair at their wedding.

Angela with her company Capri.

The Beast

With Jenny and a shop assistant in Carnaby Street.

Angela enjoying a drink at Tymawr.

A Bellfax Sales Conference. Angela and Joan on either side of me, with Robin looking on. Pity we didn't take heed of the notice on the wall.

In July, Cliff (remember him?) had his tenth number one with 'We Don't Talk Anymore', eleven years after his last number one (a gap that was longer than many pop singers' careers).

In July, I went up to Harrogate for the gift fair, where Angela joined me to celebrate her twenty second birthday. On my return, I tendered my resignation: in August, I accompanied Sue to the South West for four days, followed by a week's holiday.

With Angela already having departed, Joan from Wetherby tendered her resignation, and I left in September. It was the beginning of a downward spiral from which Bellfax would not recover.

In October, Angela and I went out for a meal with Bruce and his wife, then on to Leicester Square to see 'Alien'. We managed to keep our dinner down, but it was a close thing.

So, after eight years, starting as a Sales Representative, moving to Area Manager, then Sales Manager, then Sales Director, it had all come to nothing. My Sales Directorship in a very small company counted for precious little in the outside world, and my next job was as a Sales Representative for a rival firm in the giftware field. I cheered up a little at a great party at Mike's house in December, amongst the old crowd, but with Angela now on my arm.

And so the first forty years, and the book, are coming to an end. I hope I've had some interesting tales to tell but I had now moved out of the fast lane. On the plus side, I had a nine year old daughter, a twenty-two year old girlfriend and an eighty-two year old house; on the minus side, my marriage had not been a success, I was once again out of work with a C.V. that would not impress anybody, and I was finding it increasingly expensive to run the Beast without a salary and an expense account.

My fortieth birthday, however, turned out to be most unusual and very enjoyable. Angela and I were invited to Terry and Sue's house for dinner, where we were joined by Jill and Blair, and Kate and Tommy. After the well lubricated meal, we all settled down to watch Koo Stark in a soft-core porn film entitled 'Emily' and Tommy was bold enough to offer Angela the chance of starring in a similar film. She declined, and I was presented with a book entitled 'The Great Lover' by A. E. Russell Shelton, the pages of which were all blank except two, which contained a couple of photos that you would think twice before showing them to your maiden aunt . . .

Epilogue

Later in the year, at Mike's instigation, I converted Rockville into two self-contained flats, and sold the ground floor flat immediately. Angela and I decided to tie the knot, and were married in the June of 1981. We then sold the first floor flat, and bought a house in Langley, in Berkshire, to be nearer Angela's office, where she was going great guns with Rank Xerox. Serena was born in May, 1983, and we moved to Redhill in 1986. Lucinda was born in September, 1988. I became self-employed and the business became successful enough for Angela to join me, and we formed a partnership and a Limited Company that exist to this day. To cap it all, I became a I became a grandfather in 2000.